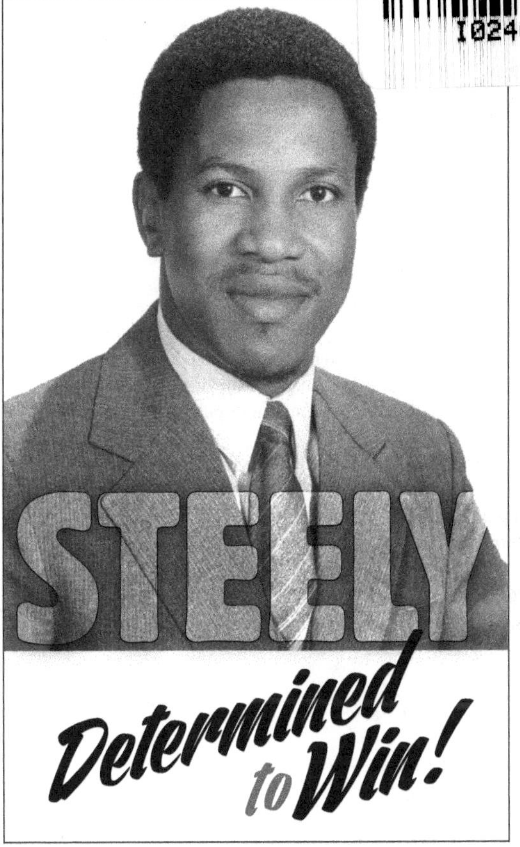

STEELY
Determined to Win!

LEOPOLD WILLIAMS, JP

Copyright © 2014 Leopold Williams.
All Rights Reserved. No part of this publication may be reproduced, stored in a retrieval system or transmitted in any form or by any means, electronic, mechanical, photocopying, recording or otherwise without the permission of author or publisher.

NATIONAL LIBRARY OF JAMAICA CATALOGUING-IN-PUBLICATION DATA

Williams, Leopold 'Steely'
   Steely: determined to win / Leopold 'Steely' Williams
   p. ; cm.
ISBN 978-976-95693-0-0 (pbk)
1. Williams, Leopold   2.   Life insurance agents – Jamaica
3. Jamaica – Biography
I. Title
368.32092 - dc 23

Executive Editor: Lena J. Rose

Copy Editor: Michelle Neita

Book layout and cover design: Mark Weinberger

Published in Kingston, Jamaica by

minna
PRESS

www.minnapress.com

Printed in United States of America

Ordering Information
Quantity (Bulk) Sales. Special discounts are available on quantity (bulk) purchases by corporations, associations, and others.
For details, contact the publisher: sales@minnapress.com

DEDICATION

To my mother, Eliza Williams and father, David Williams,
for their determination to see me develop
into a successful individual.

To my wonderful wife Diana,
for partnering with me in life and in business.

CONTENTS

Foreword		v
Preface		ix
Chapter 1	Where It All Began	11
Chapter 2	My School Days	19
Chapter 3	Getting a Job	24
Chapter 4	Faith Restored	27
Chapter 5	New Horizons	29
Chapter 6	A Spiritual Awakening	36
Chapter 7	Kingston Beckons	42
Chapter 8	A New Dispensation	49
Chapter 9	Accomplishing the Impossible	56
Chapter 10	The Politics of Change	63
Chapter 11	Determined to Win	80
Chapter 12	The Best Is Yet To Come	92
Chapter 13	Making History in The Insurance Industry	112
Chapter 14	Mission Accomplished	117
Chapter 15	Trouble in Paradise	123
Chapter 16	The End of a Magnificent Run	136
Chapter 17	The Power of Motivation	153
Chapter 18	The Future	163
Acknowledgements		170
About the Author		172

FOREWORD

> *"I studied the lives of great men and famous women, and have found that the men and women who get to the top were those who did the jobs they had in hand, with everything they have of energy and enthusiasm and hard work."*
> —HARRY S. TRUMAN

IN THIS REMARKABLE AUTOBIOGRAPHY, Steely: Determined to Win, nowhere else could Harry Truman's words epitomize a greater truth. For the author, Leopold "Steely" Williams, is already listed among the pantheon of great and famous men.

The greatest teacher in life is experience, and some of the most enduring lessons to be learnt are those outlined in the recounting of Steely's incredible journey, a pilgrimage of great achievement and dark disappointment, a life of high mountain tops and deep valleys. His story is a pathway to triumph in which the character of a man is forged in the fires of testing, in the crucible of adversity, and then, despite those daunting challenges, such a man proceeds to crown it all with uncommon success.

As one who has had the privilege of knowing Steely for the last thirty-eight years, of recruiting and training him at Life of Jamaica, I can truly say I am a firsthand witness of his astonishing success, his indomitable courage, his determination to win and his endurance in the face of trials. Steely was a team member of a magnificent ensemble of consummate professionals that made up the illustrious, record-breaking Saint Andrew Circle Branch of Life of Jamaica, a branch that

I had the honour to found and to lead. His is a true story of "rags to riches", a real-life example of the words of Eleanor Roosevelt, "The future belongs to those who believe in the beauty of their dreams".

This book makes absorbing reading and although much of it is about his heroic exploits in the life insurance industry, Steely is painting on a far broader canvas, the portrait of life's winning principles; it is also a weaving of the tapestry of success and perseverance, of an unshakeable faith in God and in the talents of entrepreneurism and selling that his Creator gave him. But talent alone could not have done it; Steely added to this the qualities of perseverance, determination and vision. One of the things I remember about Steely at Life of Jamaica (now Sagicor Life Jamaica) was something I saw unique about him—"the fierce urgency of now", as Dr Martin Luther King Jr. puts it. In the branch, whenever there was a competition, he seized the moment. He seemed to say, "If not now, when? If not I, who?" Then before others could blink he had breasted the tape—yet another trophy added to his huge collection of cups, plaques and awards. It is as if his DNA had winning as its most powerful biochemistry. In fact, as Usain Bolt is today rewriting the script on sprinting, Steely was in those days rewriting the book on selling. We used to tell agents (as they were called then) that one hundred applications in a year was the stuff of genuine success. But he was writing that number in one month! He was redefining the possible, smashing every record left, right and centre, and showing that whatever the mind of man can conceive and believe, it can achieve. In my years of management I had never seen selling with such elegant ferocity. And in doing so he was repeating for us the timeless words of George Bernard Shaw; "You see things; and you say, "Why?" But I dream of things that never were, and I say, "Why not?"

In the chronicling of his remarkable life, you will become aware of lessons that can teach us all how to succeed. You will read of how someone with only the dream and intense desire can build a successful motor car rental empire from "zero capital". You will see that instinctive quality of vision—the ability to look ahead and solve tomorrow's problems today, of buying equities and real estate when they are low in value, of seizing the moment in Jamaica's economic downturn to buy when others were selling in panic. Leopold and other visionaries profited when so many left Jamaica in fear of "socialism", leaving their properties to be bought for pennies on the dollar. This is a story of wise money management, of saving first and spending last, of strength of cash, of buying cheap, holding and selling dear (a classic axiom of wealth creation).

Winning is the coming together of many things—the dream, the hard work, the harvest and yes, the "lucky breaks". The one thing that many look curiously at and without understanding, however, is how a man or woman goes from failure to success, from good to great, and as in Steely's case, from great to phenomenal. The binding chemistry in all of this is important and it is often overlooked and unseen; it is an indispensable ingredient of winning in life. It is called persistence. Great things are not achieved without persistence. Napoleon Hill was right when he said, "There may be no heroic connotation to the word "persistence", but the quality is to the character what carbon is to steel."

"Steely" Williams is a man of steel, one who succeeded against the odds. If he did, so can you. I began this foreword with a quotation from the 33rd president of the United States. I end it with a quotation from the 32nd president, Theodore Roosevelt, for it describes the character of a winner, the measure of the man Steely, this son of St. Ann:

> The credit belongs to the man who is actually in the arena, whose face is marred by dust and sweat and blood; who strives valiantly; who errs and comes short again and again, who knows the great enthusiasms, the great devotions, and

spends himself in a worthy cause; who at the best, knows the triumph of high achievement; and who at the worst, if he fails, at least fails while daring greatly, so that his place shall never be with those cold and timid souls who know neither victory nor defeat.

Enjoy this book, and learn from a living legend who was determined to win.

D. A. Tony Williamson, CLU, ChFC, Th.M, JP
Former President and CEO,
Crown Eagle Life Insurance Company
Author, <i>The Courage to Conquer</i>

PREFACE

I DECIDED TO WRITE THIS BOOK to share my life experiences with everyone who is experiencing difficult times in their life to inspire them to find hope for their future. I have shared the story of my journey in the insurance industry at many conferences and retreats and was encouraged to put my experiences in print. I have had extraordinary success in the Life Insurance industry over the last forty years and I share them with you here.

I encourage you to read this book and hope it will help you to realize your dreams in life. Dream big, but dream with your eyes wide open, so as to see the opportunities that are emerging. What I have written in these pages gives some insight into the many struggles and disappointments I had to overcome to succeed in my chosen career. It was my determination to win that helped me to overcome all my fears.

All of this could not be possible without my faith in the Lord Jesus Christ. It was through His wisdom and enabling that I garnered the strength to go through some of the difficult experiences I have shared in this book. He taught me that when the outlook in life appears bleak, I should try the "uplook"! I always was guided by the story of Joseph in Genesis 39. He was sold as a slave in Egypt and quickly discovered he would have to learn to deal with the Pit, Potiphar, Prison and Pharaoh to reach his goal. He dealt with all these obstacles and was appointed as president of the most powerful country in the world at that time. With God, nothing is impossible.

I have tried my best to write an accurate account of what has transpired in my life over the past sixty years. While I cannot boast of any proficiency in writing, it is the determination I used to succeed in the life insurance business that I have employed here to write this book. My hope is that when you read and study the many quotes, you will find that many situations in your life change for the better. Turn the page and let's get started.

Leopold "Steely" Williams, JP

CHAPTER 1
WHERE IT ALL BEGAN

ON A DRIZZLY OCTOBER MORNING in 1952, my mother gave birth to her penultimate child, and named me, Leopold Williams. As you can see, there is no middle name as in those days it was not customary to give a middle name to a new-born child. I was the seventh child for my mother and the eleventh for my father.

Our sizeable family unit lived in a little district, named Liberty Valley, located on the outskirts of Brown's Town in Jamaica's Garden Parish, St Ann. Named after Hamilton Brown, a wealthy 19th Century property owner, Brown's Town was a Mecca for church, trade, social and educational activities. In 1952, Brown's Town was (and still is) the largest and most important inland town of the Dry Harbour Mountains.

The year, 1952, was significant for Jamaica. In the Olympics held in Helsinki, Finland, Jamaica's stellar relay team of Arthur Wint, Leslie Laing, Herbert McKenley and George Rhoden won the 4 x 400 relay, setting a world record. It was also the year that Queen Elizabeth II ascended the throne, and ruled over Britain and its Commonwealth nations, including Jamaica.

In the 50s, going to church was almost mandatory for children in the community, and having a Christian mother made it an imperative. My siblings and I started at the Brown's Town Tabernacle Church where my mother was a member. We later convinced my parents that we would prefer to attend the Baptist Church in Brown's Town which we thought was more to our liking. It was pastored at the time by a Canadian named John Bee. His wife Mary Bee was very involved with the life of the Church and the community and we found them both to be loving and kind. The Church had a large Sunday school with the best teachers you could find anywhere in the world.

Even though my father never attended church, we still had to go. On one particular Sunday morning, my cricket team was playing in a match in Trelawny. I was eager to participate. I woke up early that morning crying, "I have a belly ache".

My mother sympathized with me but my father saw through my stunt and declared: "Give him a dose of cerasee tea"—a brew that's bitter, to the taste, but supposedly cures a belly ache. The next thing I knew I drank the tea and was on my way to church.

The 50s and early 60s were very exciting times in Jamaica. These were heady days when this little island-colony of Great Britain, after nearly 200 years of African enslavement, followed by a period of Crown Colony and then Self-Government, negotiated its political independence. I was still a young boy in my tenth year when we gained our political independence from Britain, and I still have vivid memories of everyone celebrating. Even at that tender age, it was clear to me that there was a consciousness that we could take care of our own destiny. We also witnessed the emergence of our own culture, with Ska being the popular music form at the time. I loved the music and could identify every artist who had a song on the radio—from the Skatalites to Prince Buster, Derrick Morgan and many more.

In those days, few Sound Systems existed. We were fortunate to have one in my backyard that was called "King Edwards and Trojan". This was owned by Mr. Jerry Edwards, the owner of a major shop in our district. I used to hang around the disc jockey, Phillip, now deceased, and he would allow me to spin some of the records. On any given weekend, all the villagers would gather in the street and we would have a lot of fun dancing.

The Jamaica Broadcasting Corporation (J.B.C.), one of the two radio stations at the time, had an outdoor broadcast programme where they would go around the country and organize dance competitions. The name of the programme was "The Teenage Dance Party," hosted by Uriel Aldridge and the legendary Beverley Anderson, who later married the fourth prime minister of our independent nation, Michael Manley.

Brown's Town was not to be left out of these island-wide broadcasts due to it being an important market town in St Ann, and well known for its established high schools in and around the vicinity—York Castle, St Hilda's, Westwood, and Servite Convent. When the radio hosts arrived for the show in Addison Park, a centre for major events in Brown's Town, the venue was packed to capacity.

Many people urged me to compete in the dance competition. Even though I was a good dancer, I was very shy, and dancing in public was the last thing I wanted to do. However, I must confess that the prize of £4 and a few crates of my favourite aerated water drinks from Desnoes and Geddes proved compelling.

I eventually yielded to my friend's goading and joined with my partner. Sixty couples competed for the coveted prize. My partner and I danced our way into the hearts of the patrons and we emerged as winners. I took my winnings home to my mother and she took all of it and bought a Bible and a dictionary for the start of the school term. Her actions showed me that I needed to focus on The Bible and on learning rather than showing off in public. I was more than a little disappointed that I did not get more from my prize though.

Living Conditions

I spent all of my childhood years in the same community of Liberty Valley where I was born. Located just outside the main commercial centre of Brown's Town, it was not considered the suburbs. That was reserved for areas like Minard Hill to the west which was a residential area for the wealthy. The Minard Estate was known for sugar, and cattle estates and also producing various crops such as pimento. Today, the last vestiges of our local colonial history can be seen by viewing the New Hope Great House and the Minard Great House ruins. To the south was Huntley which also had vast properties. To the east was Aberdeen where all the judges, lawyers and successful businessmen lived. Liberty Valley, however, was a small farming community, having an informal record of having the most bars per square foot. It was a regular feature on weekends to see men staggering on the roads, haunted by Mr Wray and his nephew; Jamaica's famous white rum, J. Wray & Nephew.

We lived in a three-bedroom house which was far superior to what existed in the community. I grew up with three sisters and three brothers. I had other brothers, one from my mother before she was married and four from my father but they did not live with us. A very close family, my three sisters were all older than my three brothers and I. My sisters were in charge when my parents were away. During the holidays from school, we all had to help on the farm. My father was very strict and we were not able to stay out late at nights.

The only entertainment in Brown's Town during my childhood was the movie theatre, now occupied by the town's bus park. We were not allowed to go to the movies and disobeying my father's rules would mean sleeping outside the house. Whenever a Western was being shown, my brothers and I would defy my father and go to the theatre. When we arrived home, my sisters would open the windows and sneak us in.

Our parents taught all of us to work hard and instilled in us from an early age that honesty and fair play were necessary ingredients for success in life. We have all held onto this and all my siblings have gone on to do well in their chosen fields of work.

WITH MY BROTHERS AND SISTER (FROM LEFT) LLOYD, MYSELF, DIMPLE, CLAUDE, VINCENT, TERRENCE. NOTE: TWO BROTHERS AND TWO SISTERS NOT PICTURED, AND TWO SIBLINGS DECEASED.

Even though we owned our own home, we grew up under poor conditions. Being a family of eleven children, there wasn't enough money to spread around for things like education, clothing and all the other things that we would have liked to have.

I felt that my family situation wasn't so bad after I read about three successful persons who described how poor they were:

1. One man said he was so poor that even the rats had to eat next door as there were no leftovers for them.

2. James Brown, arguably, one of the greatest entertainers of all time, said his parents were so poor that they gave him the same meals every day; namely oatmeal, cornmeal and no meal.

3. Another man said that his family was so poor that they could only afford three illnesses in their family: mumps, measles and chicken pox, and his mother would cure all of them with Epsom salt.

My father the disciplinarian

My father, David Williams, was slim and handsome. He was a farmer as well as a butcher by profession. He had seemingly followed the family tradition as both his parents were farmers. He did most of the farming on seven acres of land in Orange Hill, where he was born, an area situated on the eastern side of Brown's Town. It was roughly six miles from where our family home was located. As early as I can recall, my father would have me and my siblings, work the farm during the holidays. On weekends, while my friends were having fun, my father chose me to accompany him to sell in the market because I demonstrated good money management skills.

Even though my father could not give us everything we wanted, we could not ask anyone else for money or beg or borrow anything from our friends at school. He was a proud man. If we dared to beg or borrow, and he found out, we would have to return it to the lender's home, regardless of the time of night. It was from those experiences that I learnt to live within my means and that there was an honest way out of any situation that I was faced with in life.

My early years were difficult. Many mornings I had to walk six miles to the farm with my brothers to milk the cows. We would supply the milk truck and then take the rest home for our family. My father was a disciplinarian and definitely did not take no for an answer. As children, we knew not to disobey him or we'd suffer the consequences. He was hardworking and disciplined and did everything he could that was honest to take care of his family.

Although I grew up under strict rules as a child, this did not stop me from partaking in the antics typical of a child. Our district was surrounded by larger properties and we would quite frequently raid the orange and mango trees. I would do this with the hope that my parents would not get the slightest word that I participated or I would be walking uncomfortably for quite a few days.

My Beloved Mother

My mother, Eliza Williams, was light-skinned in complexion or a "browning" as some would say in today's Jamaica. She grew up across the street from where our house was situated.

Even though she was intelligent, she was not privileged to complete her schooling. She would often tell us that she was only able to complete "third book", the usual reference to Third Standard or Grade 9. Some time ago, I was fortunate enough to see one of the letters she would mail to her family members in England. Her handwriting was impeccable. She wrote all the letters for her brothers and sisters. She was also asked to bank and manage all money that was sent home by her brothers who had settled abroad. The money was deposited in the bank and there was never an accusation about any being missing.

As I mentioned before, my mother was blessed to have eight children, seven from her marriage with my father and one from a prior relationship. She also had the responsibility of raising four other children my father had before he married her. She was hardworking and committed to my father by being involved in whatever business or other tasks he would take on. My father was also very committed to her as well, and I have never heard of him ever being involved in any extra-marital affair.

My mother was a dressmaker by profession and used to sew for the entire family. She passed on this skill to her three daughters who are all very good fashion designers. My mother wanted to work but my father insisted that she stay home and take care of the family. She did this with pride and dignity and today we are the beneficiaries of good quality parenting.

Her parents were Christians so she had a very strict Christian upbringing. Her parents were members of the Brown's Town

Tabernacle Church, led by a white Canadian Missionary by the name of Dr Kennedy. We were actually born in the church as the class house, as it was called in those days, was situated in my mother's yard, next door to the family house. Unfortunately, I did not know my mother's father who I learnt was a spiritual giant in his time. I was, however, very fortunate to have grown up next door to the only grandparent I knew, my grandmother.

If ever there was a Christian, my grandmother was one. My grandmother had long straight hair, and was very beautiful in every way. I was blessed to be the person who was selected from amongst my siblings to read the Bible to her. I can recall sitting on her big four-poster bed, reading her favourite scriptures to her. She would often put her hands on my head and pray for me. She always told me that one day I was going to be a great man, a moment I am still waiting on. There were also aunts and uncles living there who would enforce any disciplinary measures that my parents meted out.

CHAPTER 2
MY SCHOOL DAYS

I MUST CONFESS that my days in school are one part of my life I would have liked to be different. However, it was the great man Booker T. Washington, founder of the Tuskegee University who said:

> I have learned that success is to be measured not so much by the position that one reached in life but by the obstacles which he has to overcome while trying to succeed.

The state of our school system in 1958 when I started to attend Infant School was much different than what is the norm today. In those days, children stayed at home and did not start school until they were about six years old. We also didn't have a choice of basic and early childhood institutions as we do now. We had an infant school in an area district of Brown's Town called Standfast, located approximately two miles from where we lived, and which served the entire Brown's Town area.

From my recollection, I was very anxious to start school because I could actually read and write before the age of six. The Brown's Town Infant School had some famous teachers in my time. I can remember the principal, Mrs Tucker. An excellent music teacher, she was the mother of four sons and a daughter—all now accomplished musicians. Another teacher, Mrs Blanche, was short in stature but powerful in her speech. Back then, teachers would take a personal interest in the welfare of their students and would ensure that each one attained a measure of success.

I moved from the Brown's Town Infant School to Brown's Town Primary, which was called "Park School". This school was managed by the legendary Teacher Atkinson, a Jamaican white man whose skin colour changed when he got upset. Living on the school premises as was the norm for primary school teachers, Teacher Atkinson seemed a permanent fixture. He was always at school. He taught all subjects with equal competence, and would deputise for any teacher who was absent from school.

The Primary School was also about two miles from where we lived and we had to walk there each morning, rain or shine. The school had three grades, based on ability, Grades A-C, and I was fortunate to always be in the 'A' class, among the top ten students.

We had some outstanding teachers; I must mention a few. There was Mrs Nel Wedderburn who still sings on the choir at my church. Mrs Olivene Chambers, distinguished herself among lecturers at Moneague College as a reading specialist, and went on to become principal of Brown's Town Comprehensive High School. She is regarded highly as a great educator. Mae Williams, affectionately known as "Aunt Mae", was also my teacher, and she still tries to keep abreast of every new achievement in my life. If I don't give her an update when she visits the island, I will surely be in trouble. Up to midway in my primary school years, things were going in the right direction in spite of our family's economic struggles. My parents had to make a lot of sacrifices to purchase books and provide lunch for all their children each day. There were many days when no money was available for lunch and we would have to take food from home to have something to eat during the school day. I suffered through days where hunger reached its peak. School would be in session from 9am to 5pm but the lunch I got was so small, it quieted my hunger for barely an hour.

Despite the lack of necessities, I was a very quiet and well-behaved student. I loved to play and was always on the playing field. I would never miss a game of my favourite sport, cricket. Our cricket bats were either a piece of the coconut brow or a piece of board, nothing fancy. I was a good athlete and represented my school many times during my tenure there.

While in primary school, an incident occurred which branded me for the rest of my life. My good behaviour was sorely put to the test by a fellow who terrorised all the students. He was always involved in fights and would win them too. Since I was so laid back, I was not expected to engage the school bully in a fight.

One day the bully picked a fight with me. He pinned me on to the fenced wall. I managed to release his grip and shoved him back against the wall. I pummeled him with my fists while all the other students watched.

In the ensuing months I enjoyed hero status. I had tamed the bully and he never bothered any of the students again. The bully and I became good friends after our encounter and today he is a born-again Christian. From this incident, I was named "Steelman", hence the name "Steely".

Back then it was the norm for children in my village to go to school barefooted, but wearing short pants was something we 'graduated from' by age 11. I had too long a run in these short pants and at age 13, I protested to my father, via my mother, for him to allow me to move up to long pants.

Whether in short or long pants, my education progressed smoothly and I continued to do well. I was preparing for the Common Entrance Exam. If I passed the assessments, I could receive a scholarship to attend high school. It was a chance to change my future by opening doors into higher institutions of learning and developing a career.

With all these plans going through my mind, everything suddenly changed.

News came that fire had destroyed the main building of the school. This could not have happened at a worse time. I stayed home for a few months before the government could find a suitable alternative. They found it in Minard Hill, at the home of a retired teacher. Unfortunately, space was limited, causing the learning environment to be a challenging one. This was a very difficult period. We had to walk up a very steep hill each morning, approximately two miles away from where we lived. It is fair to say that this was where I lost my way academically and consequently I failed the exam.

I was devastated because I really wanted to move on to high school in order to pursue my life's goal – to become a teacher. At that time, the Common Entrance Examination was the ticket, especially for children in rural Jamaica to attend traditional high schools. All the hopes of poor children hinged on one exam. It was 'do or die'; a lot of pressure placed on 11-year-old children.

When I missed the opportunity to sit the Common Entrance Examination, I lost interest in school for a while. It was not until I transferred to The Brown's Town Comprehensive High School, where I really began to get serious again. Students did not need to pass the Common Entrance Exams to attend this school. I was fortunate to have some brilliant teachers who showed a lot of interest in me. I then sat the Technical School Examinations and succeeded.

My success in the technical schools examination also afforded me a scholarship for an agricultural school. Both scholarships would mean living in another part of the island. My father was going through some serious financial difficulties. As the sole breadwinner, he informed me that he would be unable to send me to either school.

Seeing this as the end of my academic pursuits, I was devastated yet again.

At the end of the academic year, at the age of sixteen, I left school. I felt like a ship without a rudder. I had no set goals. My dear mother, however, would not allow me to drift, and she insisted that I go back to school, this time for evening classes. She did everything that was possible to find the money to pay for these lessons.

CHAPTER 3
GETTING A JOB

AFTER ATTENDING EVENING SCHOOL, I now wanted to go to college to become a teacher. My friend and I spent a lot of time under a naseberry tree at his home, to study the subjects that were needed to enter college.

I learnt from a family friend that the Kaiser Bauxite Company, now owned by Noranda, was recruiting seven young men to send to the College of Art, Science and Technology (CAST), now the University of Technology. He told me he was going to submit my name to be interviewed for the prize.

I couldn't sleep as anxiety and excitement flooded my mind.

In the 60s and 70s, Kaiser, and no doubt the other bauxite companies in rural Jamaica, was the place to work. People came from far and wide with the hope of landing a job, as these international corporations were the highest paying employers of the time. A Mr Linton, the superintendent in charge of the Tobolski Plant, called me for an interview.

I sat the test and waited expectantly for the call.

The call came, but with it more disappointment. That week I developed what I thought was influenza. I was in bed when a telegram came for me to report to work. I was unable to take the job.

For six months, and even after many visits to the doctor, I had this mystery illness that baffles me to this day. Eventually, I got back on my feet and was able to resume classes. I was determined to be a teacher.

In the interim, I got a part-time job with the parish council office in Brown's Town as a field assistant. I supervised men in the cleaning and paving of parochial roads. I had a lot of fun with these men, supervising and eating some of the good country-style cooking they dished out to me each day. But this was not what I wanted. I eagerly hoped for something better.

On one particular evening it seemed like my days of disappointment were about to end. I was sitting at home when I heard that the manager of the only printery in town, Max Print Limited, was outside to see me. He had come to offer me a job at his printing business. In those days, a printery was regarded highly, and there weren't any computers yet. This printery had some of the major contracts for the hotels and businesses in Jamaica. I saw no reason to decline the offer. Another plus was that it was just around the corner from where I did evening studies.

Long were the hours at the printery, but we earned good money through overtime pay, and I was able to use this money to purchase some of the things I needed and pay for my studies. After one year on the job, my dream of being a teacher persisted. I had completed my exam and awaited the results. But again, more disappointment. I failed English, the vital subject I needed in order to apply for college. I now felt like this was definitely the end and to make matters worse, my friend and study partner passed the test and was on his way to Sam Sharpe Teacher's College in St James. Suffice to say, I was crushed.

Despondent, I became withdrawn and did not speak to anyone unless it was necessary. I stopped going to church and became rebellious. Night life became my outlet, and I would frequent out-of-town parties and dances even if I had to walk back home.

A feeling of helplessness and apathy washed over me. I drank, gambled and cursed, all the time knowing that my life was heading in the wrong direction. I had the consciousness that there was a God and that he could help me, but frustration and despair got the better of me.

CHAPTER 4
FAITH RESTORED

IN MARCH OF 1973, A FRIEND SUGGESTED that I accompany him to visit two young ladies, so I went along. Our mission was aborted prematurely however, as their parents came home early. I got home to discover that everyone had gone to the Brown's Town Baptist Church where an evangelistic crusade was in progress. This fiery preacher had come to my old church but I had no interest. That evening, I decided to take a walk up there just to see what was going on.

I sneaked in, took a back seat and enjoyed the singing, but had made up my mind that as soon as the preaching started I would make my exit. This never happened though, for as Reverend Lindsey Moncrieffe started to deliver the message, I became captivated.

Did someone tell him about my life story? I wondered. Everything he said seemed to apply directly to my experiences. That night, I decided to surrender my life to the Lord. I also did something that was very uncharacteristic of me. I made the walk through the aisles of the church, went to the front, and at that moment I felt like a new man. A feeling of hope came over me again as I read the Bible and attended Bible Studies, sharing and fellowshipping with the brethren. In September of 1973, I was baptised and became a member of the church.

It was in that same month that I got my driver's license. This was a great achievement at the time as there were few young men at the age of twenty-one who possessed a driver's license. By that time, my father's fortunes changed and he now owned a motor vehicle which he was able to purchase with cash. He, however, would not allow me to drive it as he was fearful that my youthful exuberance would lead me to crash his car.

On the night of my conversion, the Lord gave me a scripture and made a promise to me— *"Seek ye first the Kingdom of God and all these things will be added onto you."* (Matthew 6:33). This verse gave me a new confidence that my life would turn around and it now seemed like my journey of disappointment was about to take a new path.

CHAPTER 5
NEW HORIZONS

"Sometimes people think its holding on that makes one strong, sometimes its letting go." —SYLVIA ROBINSON

N 1973, I WAS STILL WORKING at the printery and had received a good increase in pay, but I told the Lord that this was not what I wanted and I knew he would answer my prayer. I had no idea where the Lord would take me but I was willing to follow. It was after a Sunday morning service that same year that a church brother stopped me on my way out of church. He wanted to talk to me about an employment opportunity that was available in the insurance company with which he was associated.

I did not allow him to finish before I said: "No, no! Such a career is reserved for people who are eloquent and convincing. I do not feel I fit that profile". I'm sure anyone who knew me at the time would agree. He insisted, but when he realized he was struggling to convince me, he backed off. I chose to forget about the life insurance field as a car would be needed and I didn't see one appearing in my immediate future. A new Ford Escort, one of the least expensive cars at that time, cost $1,100. But few people my age could even think of owning one.

I spent my evenings at the York Castle High School playing cricket. On one such evening, I was interrupted by my friends who told me there was a gentleman in the parking lot who wanted to see me. I went out and saw two well-dressed men along with my church brother. He was adamant that he wanted me to represent his company in the area as he was about to retire. It did not take much time to see that the manager was driving one of my favourite cars, a

124 Sport Fiat. I looked at it in amazement and started to think, "I could be driving one soon!" As much as I tried, I could not escape the recruiting efforts of the two gentlemen, Ralph Khaleel who was the regional manager, and Trevor Jones, the branch manager at the Ocho Rios office. They convinced me to begin studying for the insurance licensing exams. I sat and passed the examination in January of 1974 which perhaps signalled the beginning of a change in my fortunes.

An intensive three-month training course, conducted by Mr Khaleel of British Fidelity Insurance Company, began. The head office was situated in Jacksonville, Florida and they operated in about eighteen different territories.

Back then, many of the insurance companies operating in Jamaica marketed industrial insurance. They sold mainly to people who were paid weekly, and similarly, their premiums would be collected by their agents on a weekly basis.

An agent would be required to sell policies each week and collect what was described as the debit. Anyone who knows about this area of the insurance industry would know that this is one of the most difficult areas of business one could enter.

The agent had to possess expert selling skills to survive and achieve any measure of success. I was asked to present a list with names of persons whom I could approach to sell policies in my first month. By the time I had completed my list I had just about made up my mind to quit. After all, I did not own a motor car, and going on foot seemed almost impossible; never mind the fact that many of the agents had no car.

The 1st of April, 1974 marked the beginning of my contract as an agent of the company. My first prospect was my cousin's wife, and while I knew her very well, I was trembling when I knocked on her door. I went in and explained the need for her to buy insurance and was very happy when she purchased.

I began to feel that this business of selling insurance was easy. In the months that followed, I did extremely well. The Manager of the Ocho Rios Branch was happy and told me, "You are going to be a star in the insurance industry".

At this time, I still did not have a car and I didn't know if I would be able to continue without one.

To my surprise, my manager went to my home the next day to see my father to try and convince my father to buy a car for me. I thought he was on an impossible mission but again to my surprise he emerged as the winner.

He somehow got my father to spend all the money he had in the bank on a used car so that I could continue selling insurance for his company.

I had mixed feelings about this. While I was happy that I now owned a car—a rarity for people of my age and race at that time—the risk of failure weighed heavily on me.

What if I failed?

What would my father say?

I was left with one option, I had to succeed.

MY FIRST CAR AT AGE 21

I worked very hard for long hours, calling everyone who could buy my products. I continued to do extremely well, and at the end of 1974, I won several awards for excellence in selling the most cases in the company. I was now among the top earners in the company but, for me, being the number one was what would bring me the most happiness.

In 1975, I was perhaps the youngest person in the company as there was a minimum age limit of 25 for persons seeking to enter the industry. It was felt that persons below that age did not possess the sense of responsibility to be employed in a field which required so much discipline.

I was just twenty-two years old but I was disciplined and had learned the value of hard work from my father who never left me out of his business plans.

Despite my young age, I set out to be the number one agent in the company that year. Some of my older colleagues thought I was crazy, but I remained focused. There is a quote by someone that says "whether you think you can or you think you can't, you are dead right." I set out to do what some people thought was impossible. I worked long days, on weekends and holidays and broke several company records in the process.

In those days, there wasn't any free flow of information, as it is today; to show how near or far we were from other competing agents. At the end of the year, the final results were announced and I was declared second in the company, losing by the narrowest of margins. If I had known my competitor was that near he could never have won.

Despite that, I was very happy for what was happening in my career and I was now among the best in the business. My manager was happy, the head office in Kingston was happy and, as a result, people began to take greater notice of me.

In 1976, I was invited to the Company's Awards Banquet in San Juan, Puerto Rico where I was presented with the Runner-up Trophy in the entire company. I felt tremendous satisfaction with that achievement.

Prior to leaving the country I was given the huge sum, at the time, of $500 JMD which I exchanged for US$600. This allowed me to have a good time shopping in the city of San Juan. How I long for a

BRITISH FIDELITY MANAGER, TREVOR JONES PRESENTS AN AWARD TO ME

return of the days when the Jamaican Dollar has more value than the United States Dollar. While at the convention, I discovered that there were some rewards that I should have been getting that weren't forthcoming. I had an old car that spent more time in the garage than on the road, so I spoke to management about getting a new car in order to increase my productivity.

My manager promised he would speak to head office (the nebulous term we used in reference to our seemingly nameless, faceless corporate decision makers) about the matter.

A few weeks later, he informed me that head office was lending me the money to buy a new car.

With the possibility of owning a reliable car now on the horizon, I was very excited about the prospect of topping the company in sales in 1976, and I knew I could do it.

I advertised my car for sale, now very delighted that I was going to be able to drive what I dreamt about in my early years, a brand new car.

My car sold for the good price of a thousand dollars, and I was preparing to make a down payment on the new car when my manager brought me some bad news. He said, "The Company has ceased its policy of lending money to sales representatives to purchase cars".

Overcome with devastation and demotivation, I later learnt that the company had nothing to do with that decision as it was my manager and his assistant manager who were behind it. They thought that if I got a new car I would have a better profile in the branch than they had, and they would have none of this idea of me driving a new Rover.

I had held on to some ideas all my life, and I was determined that nothing would stop me from actualising them. I thought very seriously about what was happening to me and decided that these were not people with whom I would want to entrust my future. I understood that it was not advisable to leave the job without having a suitable alternative in place, but I discussed it with my church elders. I prayed to the Lord and asked him to guide my decision as I could not go back to where I was coming from.

The Lord truly works in mysterious ways.

Not long after my prayer, my adopted spiritual mother, Sister Ivy Marston, invited me to her house where I usually enjoy some good country style cooking. She told me she had a message from the Lord for me. The Lord had told her I was not happy with my job and that I should leave my job. Although I prayed, it was still difficult to make the decision as I had now secured a loan to buy a fairly new Ford Escort in my favourite colour, yellow.

I had moved out of my parent's house and now lived in Cardiff Hall in a five bedroom house that I shared with a friend. I had saved some money in the bank and I believed I would be able to manage until the next job came. I had now come to the conclusion that I would not want to ever pursue a career in the life insurance industry. I figured I could use the money I had saved to complete my education, so I wrote my letter of resignation and gave it to my manager.

They tried to persuade me to stay but by then I had come to the realisation that this was not where the Lord wanted me to be.

My Decision to Leave the Insurance Industry

By this time the news reached the head office and Mr Ralph Khaleel, who was my trainer and now Director of Agencies, called to say he was disappointed. By then, we had a good relationship and I explained my reason for leaving. He asked me if I wanted to re-join the company, and offered to promote me to a management position at the Mandeville Branch.

I did not take the offer as I had fixed my mind on not being involved with insurance business in my future endeavours. Later in life, Mr Khaleel and I developed a close relationship as we were members of the Kingston Cricket Club and would see each other whenever a match was played at Sabina Park. He always expressed that he was not surprised at what I achieved at Life of Jamaica as he had seen it in me on the very same day I stepped into his class for training.

CHAPTER 6
A SPIRITUAL AWAKENING

> *"Education is not preparation for life, education is life itself."* — JOHN DEWEY

DURING MY TIME in the insurance business, I would never work on a Sunday as was required at the time by the company. I attended church every Sunday and played an active role. Many people who attended church did not own cars, so most Sunday mornings I would drive preachers to different churches to preach.

It was around this time that Vincent Reid and I developed a close friendship while I drove him to various places to preach the gospel. I was not given the call to be a preacher but I would share in other ministries.

By late 1976, my savings were depleted and I was back in the old position of trying to get a job. None was forthcoming and I got worried, but I was not prepared to go back to my previous way of living. Meanwhile, Vincent had gotten a job and he assisted in maintaining the car.

I am now convinced that the Lord moved me from the insurance business to straighten out my spiritual life. It was during that period that the Charismatic Movement was sweeping across North America and entering Jamaica, and I had time on my hands to cultivate a hunger for the Word.

I would journey with a group in my car to Kingston on Saturday mornings to share in fellowship at the Sheraton Kingston Hotel's ballroom. Most mornings I would wake up with no money to purchase gasoline, but the Lord always provided a way to get the vehicle to and from Kingston.

My Second Call to Duty

I had sold my Ford Escort and purchased an older and less valuable model so that I could keep the equity for living expenses. I moved back to my parent's residence and my life was swiftly returning to where it had begun.

One afternoon, I was hanging out at the Esso Service Station, at the entrance to Brown's Town, when a Peugeot motor car drove up and parked by the Jamaica Agricultural Society Branch. The car was driven by Mr Desmond Smith, manager at the powerful Mutual Life Assurance Society.

Mr Smith was a very successful and knowledgeable insurance man. Managers from my previous office used to attend classes which Mr Smith instructed and which were held at his office in the beautiful building located at the centre of Ocho Rios. He knew about my exploits at British Fidelity Insurance Company and came over to have a chat with me and advised me to return to the business.

I really didn't want to hear anything of the sort, but I listened.

He was on his way to Alexandria to see his old acquaintances, the Walford family, and he asked me if I would come for a ride to discuss a career at Mutual Life.

I had nothing else to do, so I went for the ride in his luxury car.

He explained what a contract with Mutual Life would do for me and went on to inform me that he was conducting a class at his home in Huntley, Brown's Town, with two other prospective recruits. He encouraged me to join them. Even though I resisted, he eventually won me over.

For some weeks, he instructed us in preparation for the Ordinary Long Term Insurance Examination set by the Office of the Superintendent of Insurance and administered by the hard-nosed Harold Milner. The successful completion of the course was a pre-requisite for obtaining a contract to sell Ordinary Long Term insurance policies.

I have always believed that education was my only way out of my many failures. I was determined to enrol in a tertiary institution at any cost. With that in mind, I studied the text, sat the examinations at the Old Library on the Mona Campus of the University of the West Indies. Within a few weeks, I got the news that I was successful in the examination.

A sense of the possibilities invaded my mind once again, but that was to be a pipe dream. I was asked to complete several assignments during what is referred to as the pre-contract period, in preparation for an interview. In those days, all prospective applicants for a sales job had to visit the company's head office in Kingston to be interviewed by a selection panel. Four months had passed since the time of preparation for the examination and the pre-contract period. I was getting very impatient and I expressed my disappointment to my recruiting manager, Mr Smith.

On a visit to the Ocho Rios Branch it became evident that there wasn't anyone in sales there who were in my age group or who had my academic experience. As a result, I wasn't that surprised when Mr Smith informed me that I wasn't selected to work with the company. After all the hard work he had done he was just as disappointed as I was.

Perhaps because of that disappointment, perhaps because he wanted to offer me a better quality of life, or both, Mr Smith and his wife invited me to move in with them and to live with their family. I pondered whether I should accept the invitation. You see, they had not yet given their lives to Christ, and I had grown to be very serious about my beliefs and how I lived. I prayed about the matter and I got the go ahead from the Lord who I knew would be with me.

I moved into a very large room on the ground floor of their house. They treated me like family and this was the beginning of what turned out to be over 35 years of close friendship. Subsequently, they visited my church and both became born again Christians. Mr Smith was first, followed by his wife, Mauva. He went on after retirement from Mutual Life to attend the United Theological College of the West Indies and was ordained as a Baptist minister. He served in two church circuits in Trelawny and Bethany, respectively. He is now retired but very active in the Brown's Town Baptist Church. Even though he was not successful in getting me to join Mutual Life, he still thought I should get back into the industry.

It was now 1977, and the Charismatic Movement (a fundamentalist movement within Christian churches that emphasises the gifts of the Holy Spirit, i.e. speaking in tongues and healing of the sick) was having a great impact in our church. We continued to travel to Kingston for meetings at the Sheraton Kingston Hotel and would have a wonderful time in the Lord. Our church was also growing in numbers. Six of us who were members decided to start a fellowship at the nearby Anglican Church Hall to introduce the new experience to people in the area who weren't able to travel to the city. We would meet each Saturday morning for fellowship and then the six of us would meet again in the week for discussion, feedback and to plan our next meeting.

This period had a great impact on my Christian life and came to be very useful in my life in the insurance business. It was around that time that I forged a good relationship with the Torado Heights Christian Centre in Montego Bay. We had some great spiritual experiences there with Menzie Oban, the pastor, and his family. I am very happy I was able to serve as a trustee and Chairman of the Finance Committee, and I will always remember the many blessings that I received in my life, blessings which have enabled me to be the person I am today.

There was a yearly Charismatic Teaching Conference where international speakers like Derek Prince, Harry Greenwood, Bob Mumford and many others would address the Conference. My pastor at the Brown's Town Baptist Church, Reverend Everard Allen, had spoken at these conferences on several occasions and had developed relationships with some of its leaders.

Tony Williamson was invited to speak at our meetings at the Church. I had heard about him through my attendance at these meetings and also through his brother-in-law Lewis Campbell. Mr Williamson delivered the message in his usual eloquent style and then gathered at the pastor's residence for repast. Desmond Smith and I had approached him to give our commendations which led to them striking up a conversation about the insurance business.

It did not take a long time to surmise that he had a clear passion for the field of insurance. He asked Desmond if he knew anyone who was interested in a career in life insurance as he was looking for someone to represent his company, Confederation Life, in Ocho Rios. Before he could finish speaking, Desmond responded that I was the man.

I wanted to tell him not to introduce me because I didn't want to work in Kingston, I knew nothing of Confederation Life and I had no further interest in the insurance field. By that time I had changed my focus to trying to acquire capital to start my own business.

Being a good life insurance man, Mr Williamson did not hesitate to take out one of his business cards and invited me to see him on the next Monday at his office in New Kingston. I pondered whether I should get back into the business and I made a few attempts to call and say I was not interested. I prayed to the Lord, "Please allow me to make the right decision as I just could not bear another failure in my life."

A thought came to me that Kingston provided most of the opportunities available where I could continue my education. I figured I could go to Kingston to earn some money to fund my education and complete this elusive dream of mine.

CHAPTER 7
KINGSTON BECKONS

"We must accept finite disappointment but we must never lose infinite hope."
—MARTIN LUTHER KING, JR

K**INGSTON WAS UNFAMILIAR TO ME.** I rarely drove so my knowledge of New Kingston was very limited. Moreover, most of my few trips there had been visiting the downtown area to watch cricket matches at Sabina Park.

I had developed a fear of being in the city. During my childhood I heard stories of the evils that transpired there. Once while I was in primary school, my mother decided to shop in Kingston for our school supplies. She met a well-dressed con-artist who took her to a store where she could supposedly get great bargains. The man stole all of her money. This event conjured a lot of fear in my mind.

With great trepidation, I headed off to Kingston. I was directed to go on Spanish Town Road, turn up Hagley Park Road, turn on Eastwood Park Road, make a right by the Jamaica Broadcasting Corporation (JBC), and go down Halfway Tree Road then on Holborn Road and finally a right to Dumfries Road. I had an old, two-door Ford Escort and I was unable to afford to get it properly serviced because I was not working at the time. During my journey, it developed a thirst for water. I had to stop on many occasions to pour water in the radiator.

I had no issues in getting to Hagley Park Road but I lost my way at the point where I should have turned at South Odeon Avenue where JBC was located. I must have gone off course about fifteen times before I finally reached Holborn Road. Eventually, I reached

Dumfries Road and easily found where the office was located. I couldn't help but notice the fabulous cars parked outside.

I knew that some life insurance underwriters were inside so I made sure that I parked further down the road. I didn't want to face the embarrassment of one of those fellows seeing the car I drove.

I went in the office and fortunately for me, Lewis Campbell, Tony's brother-in-law, saw me and brought me to Tony's office. He was enthusiastic and quickly made me feel at ease.

Uncertain that I would get the job, thoughts of my past failures swirled in my head. I wasn't dressed for the interview perhaps because I just did not care about what was going to happen.

Tony asked me a few questions and I answered them to the best of my ability. I observed that he was about to get sophisticated, being a man who is well versed in the English language. I told him that all I wanted to do was earn a lot of money. In my understanding, having a lot of money was the norm in the insurance business and I definitely planned to earn my fair share.

He called his brother-in-law who was one of his representatives and told him he was about to offer me an opportunity to represent the company in the St Ann area. He instructed him to give me one of their big leather rate books and to show me the rates and how to complete applications. I did not find it difficult as I had two years of prior experience in the industry. I looked around the office and saw some well-dressed men, with high afro haircuts, and few women, as the industry was male-dominated at the time.

I could see the looks on their faces, even though they didn't express it verbally I knew they were saying, "where is this little country boy going? He has failed already." In all fairness to them, based on my attire that day, their assessment wasn't far off the mark.

> *"A successful man is one who can lay a firm foundation with the bricks others have thrown at him."* —DAVID BRINKLEY

Confederation Life Here I Come!

Confederation Life was one of the leading life insurance companies in Canada. Their Jamaican branch was operated as a subsidiary of Grace Kennedy & Company Limited (now Grace Kennedy Group) under the name, H. Macaulay Orrett Insurance Ltd., and was led by Mr Conrad Levy. This office was located on 6 Trinidad Terrace in New Kingston.

I found myself in a spot of difficulty again as I was still living in St Ann but employed at an office seventy-five miles away. I was broke, with not even enough money to afford petrol and maintenance for my old Ford Escort. Turning to my dear mother, the one who had already given me her life in terms of the amount of sacrifices she had made so far, I knew that whatever I took on she would want to be a part of it.

Faced with financial struggles nonetheless, I tried to get some information on the commission structure on which I would be paid. I soon discovered that it was different from the way other local companies operated. Other companies paid based on a "projected commission" format where all the first year commission fees were calculated and paid up front, on the assumption that the client would pay the entire annual premium. Confederation Life offered a system that was called the "E.P." system. The name more than likely was denoted as "Enhanced Payment" but my colleagues rightfully called it "Eternal Poverty".

August of 1977 signified my first month of production as an agent with Confederation Life. Potential clients are considered the raw material in this business and to get them I did a lot of what was called "prospecting" and "cold canvassing" with everyone I knew, and I worked long hours. I soon realised that I still had the ability to "close" cases, and in that same month was able to write quite a few insurance applications.

At the Monday morning meeting, Tony announced the monthly figures with great joy. Members of the branch were in awe at my production level. There was a gentleman of Indian descent who could not believe that a rookie had accomplished so much in one month. He called me aside and expressed his congratulations, and went on to say that my performance was to be expected in the early days but that it would eventually taper off over time. This man had been in the business for years and could have been my father. He drove an old Ford Corsair which was falling apart and he was evidently trying to block my progress. I was very disappointed by his behaviour. I informed my manager about what transpired and expressed my dismay. I really did not want him to lose his job; I only wanted Tony to speak to him as he was sowing seeds of negativity in the branch. I was in the dark about what happened next but when I came back to the office the next month, I heard his contract was terminated.

> **"Stop thinking in terms of limitations and start thinking in terms of possibilities."**
> —TERRY JOSEPHSON

In September, I was again successful in achieving another very productive month based on number of applications written, and all the big names in the company started to take note of what was happening.

It was my intention to send a message that this little man from St Ann was there to rewrite the company's records. In October, my success continued and I had now created more new business than the top agent in the unit produced for the entire year—a tremendous feat.

CONFEDERATION LIFE: TONY WILLIAMSON'S UNIT

All this time, I was getting little financial compensation. The business had to go to the head office in Canada where the underwriting process was finalised before commissions could be paid. This did not deter me as I knew that in time I would be right on the money. By now, my manager, Tony, a great motivating force for our team, was throwing his billfold on the ground and daring anyone to take on his champion (me) and win. In those days, we had a friendly rivalry within the branch and we all wanted to see everybody do their best.

> *"Mediocrity knows nothing higher than itself, but talent instantly recognizes genius."*
> —SIR ARTHUR CONAN DOYLE

At the end of October, 1977, news surfaced that Confederation Life was acquired by Life of Jamaica. This was the greatest news! Earlier that year, Life of Jamaica had become the first Jamaican-owned life insurance company and the first life insurance company to be listed on the Jamaica Stock Exchange.

I stood at the back of my house and an aeroplane flew overhead, so close I could throw a stone inside. Trailing behind the plane against a blue sky was a long, blue banner, emblazoned with a bright orange sun rising over a mountainous blue Jamaican horizon with the inscription: "For a Better Life", signalling a bright, new landscape in Jamaica. The plane flew around and around, and I could not take my eyes off of it for all the promised it offered. Eventually, my neck gave up on me.

I had met some of Life of Jamaica's agents and had read a lot about its founder, R. Danny Williams. From his surname, it was clear to me that he had some pedigree. What he did for the local insurance industry, and for Jamaica, along with his leadership style, has made him an icon in this industry. Danny Williams pioneered the nationalisation of the local insurance industry by spearheading the buyout of the local, and top producing branch of North American Life Insurance Company, headquartered in Canada.

Jamaica's Independence on August 6, 1962 brought a spirit of ownership and pride, and a great sense of urgency. Everybody wanted to be involved. It brought forth a real challenge, and the feeling was evident in political, economic and cultural spheres. During the decade, we saw a Jamaican woman, Joan Crawford winning the Miss World pageant. World class musicians emerged such as Bob Marley and the Wailers, Jimmy Cliff, Desmond Dekker, Millie Small and many others. Marcus Garvey became our first national hero. Air Jamaica was established as the national airline; what pride we felt when the first flight landed on our shores! There were a lot of business breakthroughs, and in educational awareness and in the arts. The local insurance industry was not to be left out of this new wave of national spirit which our political independence fostered, and Jamaicans, many of whom now owned shares in this new publicly-listed company, were proud of Life of Jamaica.

All over the country, people were in charge of their own destinies and had the zeal for developing new projects. Many went out on a limb to discover new missions and ideas. This was spearheaded by the government of the day which was led by The Right Excellent Sir Alexander Bustamante. It was in this atmosphere that the idea of establishing a locally controlled life insurance company caught the mind of Danny Williams and his colleagues, namely Manley McAdam, Donald Davidson, Peter Rousseau, Herbert Hall and Adrian Foreman. I had the privilege of working with some of these men during the time I served at Life of Jamaica.

> **"If you want a place in the sun you've got to put up with a few blisters."**
> —ABIGAIL VAN BUREN

These founding fathers planned to use the small branch of North American Life Assurance Company of Canada (NALCO), managed by Danny Williams to form a Jamaican company. This was no easy task in those days, considering we were a small developing nation. The then Minister of Finance, Edward Seaga, encouraged them to persist. Danny Williams led many teams to Canada to negotiate with NALCO but, even after coming back empty-handed; he was determined to start the company. And this he did in June 1970, and it proved to be a national symbol of achievement as well as a source of employment for many persons who, like me, needed an opportunity to fulfil our dreams.

> **"Always remember a man is not rewarded for having a brain but for using it."** —ANONYMOUS

CHAPTER 8
A NEW DISPENSATION

IN JUNE 1970, LIFE OF JAMAICA WAS BORN with its tagline, "For a Better Life", and with Danny Williams at the helm as its first president.

Today, many persons attest to the difference this company has made in their lives. When I read that Life of Jamaica had acquired Confederation Life in 1977, I was overcome with joy just knowing that I was going to represent one of the best companies in Jamaica. I was prepared to do whatever was necessary to write my name in the annals of the company's history.

It was now December 1977 and I was making frequent trips to the Life of Jamaica head office to familiarise myself with the policies and operational procedures of my new employers. We also had to visit the Halfway Tree Branch where the training department was located. It was operated under the leadership of the well-known trainer, Gladstone Pottinger. He was a very serious man, a disciplinarian, and we would never dare to be late with any assignments, let alone late for class. At the end of December, I received the first cheque for the business I had submitted. I was very pleased with the amount. I could not believe I was paid so much for just two months of work. I left Kingston with joy in my heart, knowing that my future now looked assured.

I can recall going to the National Commercial Bank in Brown's Town to open a current account and drew cheques for months without depleting the balance. Those were the days when our currency was stronger than the United States dollar.

Life of Jamaica told us that the date of our contract would be the First of December 1977. We now had a new location as we moved to 6 Trinidad Terrace in New Kingston which was to be the place where I made my mark in the industry.

Conrad Levy was the manager and Tony Williamson was his assistant. It took some time for us to cement the relationship due to logistical issues as well as the time needed to get familiar with the new company's products.

> *"People may doubt what you say, but they will always believe what you do."* —LEWIS CASS

> *"Human excellence means nothing unless it works with the consent of God."*
> —EURIPIDES

By January 1978, I knew that the colleagues with whom I was competing were some of the best in the business. Many were university and college graduates and they would remind you of that in their own non-verbal way. I prayed several nights that God would provide me with the mental ability to do the things that were required of me. I also had the handicap of being the only person who lived so far from my office.

During the first week of January, it was customary for the unit to meet outside of the branch for a retreat. Every agent was required to verbalise what they would be doing for the ensuing year. I had long set out what I wanted to achieve in the life insurance business, and I predicted what I would do, not only for 1978 but for my entire time with the company.

Every member of the "field force" said what they wanted to achieve that year. Our branch comedian, Winston Bennett spoke of carpeting his home that's located in one of the opulent areas in Kingston. I, on the other hand, could only dream about having a little house much less to have it carpeted.

I can recall my good friend, Denzel Vaughn who was the branch mathematician, speaking about wanting to buy another house. All I could think was, "wow".

It was my time to speak.

After my exploits in the first four months of the business, I did not expect anyone to doubt what I could do. But this was not to be.

Based on the promise I got from the Lord, in Matthew 6:33 at the time of my conversion, that I should "seek Him first", I had no doubt in my mind that I would achieve what I was about to announce. *"A wise man reflects before he speaks. A fool speaks and then reflects on what he has uttered."*

In those days, I really was a shy person and did not relish speaking in situations like that. But I got up and said, "I want to buy a Mercedes Benz!"

During my time working with the first insurance company, I was privileged to visit most of the villas in Mammee Bay and Cardiff Hall in Runaway Bay, and saw some fabulous houses by the sea. I promised myself that I would own one someday.

The next vow I made, before everyone, was, "I want to buy a house near the sea!"

Then came the vow that made everyone think I must have hit my head: "I want to retire by the age of forty-five!"

I sat down amidst peals of laughter and jokes. This continued for weeks after the meeting.

The retreat was a pivotal moment for me as declaring myself in public spurred me on to achieving my dreams. Because of the way I was treated, I resolved to achieve everything I had said in that room!

I had already done my calculations and figured that at age 25, being the youngest member of the branch, I could earn enough money to complete my children's education and do all the other things I wanted, by working for the next twenty years.

It was time to get busy. I quickly defined my target market as St Ann. Since there weren't a lot of business owners I could sell to in those days, the main target would be professionals, and civil servants such as teachers and nurses.

St Ann was a lucrative market where all the companies sent their representatives to prospect. I used all the prospecting methods I knew but most of the prospects already had coverage from Mutual Life.

Many days I approached at least thirty persons with no success in getting any sales. I however, found a loophole.

I discovered that most of the people I spoke with had unfavourable experiences with their current agents. They complained that following the sale, agents did not return to offer the service that was promised. I decided to capitalize on this and created my own GASS formula to fuel my business:

GOALS + **A**TTITUDE + **S**ERVICE = **S**UCCESS.

I was determined to make a better impression on my colleagues. I did not want the undesirable label of being the branch entertainer. The first quarter ended and I managed to write a substantial amount of applications. My detractors were now taking note that I was serious about what I said at the retreat.

The second quarter saw me producing another substantial amount of applications resulting in my first Agent of the Month award in June. I was elated. I still view it every once in a while as a reminder of my start.

During this time, I had difficulties in processing business at the head office. In 1978, technology was not what it is today. We had mainframe computers at the head office where the business was processed through a complex and archaic procedure, causing lots of problems. In the end, technology and issues with branch administration slowed some of my plans to break company records.

Nonetheless, by the end of 1978, my fortunes continued to grow. I procured a substantial amount of new business which led to my distinction as the number one agent in the branch. I took home all the major awards at the Branch Awards Ceremony. I also qualified for the prestigious Million Dollar Round Table, a distinction obtained by only five percent of insurance professionals worldwide.

WINNING ALL MAJOR TROPHIES AT FIRST BRANCH AWARDS BANQUET

I had managed to write and settle over two hundred cases, a feat that finally silenced all of my detractors. It also signalled my rise from the office laughing stock to their hero. I had demonstrated belief in myself and earned the respect of all.

I went on in 1979 to Radio City, New York to attend the Annual Meeting of the Million Dollar Round Table, and rubbed shoulders with some of the best in the business. I earned a substantial amount of money in that year as I had an almost perfect conservation of my business. I was able to take care of all my back log of bills and got rid of my old Escort. I now owned a Peugeot, considered one of the finest cars of that time.

> *"A man is what he thinks about all day."*
> —RALPH WALDO EMERSON

> *"Whether you think you can or you think you can't—you're right."* —HENRY FORD

By now most of the initiation problems that the new company underwent were coming to an end. Changes were afoot. Our beloved president, the Honourable Danny Williams, had answered a call to serve in the government of Michael Manley as Minister of Industry and Commerce.

This move would have been a great sacrifice for the company at that stage of its history. He however handed the presidency of the company to Adrian Foreman, one of its founding members.

I observed that the leading agent in the company at that time, Hennis Smith, would accompany the President on most of his visits for company assignments. I was impressed with how the top agents were treated by the company.

One morning when the President came to the branch with the top agent, I made a decision that in 1979 I would be the next agent who would be on tour of duty.

It seemed like an insurmountable task as that title was skewed towards senior agents since it was the agent who earned the most money who would be the winner. It was very difficult to achieve this status in those days. The agents who had been employed for years would have built up large amounts of renewal commissions, a substantial part of an agent's total earnings in those days.

> *"The man who moves a mountain begins by carrying small stones."* —CONFUCIUS

In March 1979, the company held its Annual Awards Banquet at the Jamaica Pegasus Hotel. This was a huge and glamorous affair, attended by the Board Chairman and his Directors, divisional heads, department and other senior company personnel. Executive Vice President and company comedian, Herbie Hall, chaired the programme. He was to become my godfather or mentor at the company. Herbie Hall held the audience in a state of continuous laughter. I did not qualify for any award but I was very amused by what I witnessed. I just could not believe that a company could pay us so well for our sales and then still reward us so extravagantly.

After all the awardees were announced and given their honours, Herbie Hall prompted a very serious moment. He said, "Could Leopold "Steely" Williams stand to your feet".

My heart started to race faster than an eight cylinder engine. I thought for a while about what I must have done to deserve this. Here was the shy, timid country boy standing in the midst of dignitaries and the strongest insurance sales force in the Caribbean. Everyone turned around, fixing their eyes on me when I stood.

Herbie Hall said: "Ladies and Gentlemen, take a good look at that man. Next year when we gather here you are going to be tired of seeing his face."

I could not believe what he said. I have never asked him who set me up and I have never asked Tony Williamson if he had anything to do with it. I had a suspicion that Tony Williamson dreamed of producing the top agent in the company. I was the only agent who he thought could take him to the Promised Land.

I was now in a predicament. I could not return to the next awards banquet without delivering.

CHAPTER 9
ACCOMPLISHING THE IMPOSSIBLE

"Thinking will get us to the foot of the mountain; faith will get us to the top."

AS A TEENAGER THERE WAS ONLY ONE RADIO in the home and this was stored in my parent's room. I did not have the privilege of turning on the radio and listening to my favourite radio programme that would come on just before the evening news. on Radio Jamaica. However, I'd slip through the backdoor and listen.

The programme played an important role in the development of my thinking for my future years. The presenter of the programme was Earl Nightingale.

I can't remember all he said but I can definitely recall one statement he made that I always use when I get the opportunity to share my experiences.

He said, **"we become what we think about all day."**

I reflected on this quote. I had to believe and think about what I needed to do in the coming year.

I shared my mission with some of my colleagues but most of them told me it was not possible to win this coveted trophy. It was also the dream of over 300 underwriters in the company.

I thought about becoming Chairman of the Production Club. It carried a lot of privileges and prestige such as being part of the

President's monthly one-hour briefing where updates were given on the Company's performance. The individual was also given "Officer of the Company" status and would act as a representative for all the other agents in the company. I was determined, that in 1980, I would be the next person to sit in this position.

I knew I would have to put in long hours, but I was prepared psychologically and physically for the task. I recalled in training that if you called thirteen persons each day, at least one person may buy. I employed this strategy on a totally different scale as I must have seen fifty persons each day. It started to pay off as I managed to close a significant amount of cases.

The environment was competitive at both company and branch levels. Each Monday morning I won most of the prizes given by management, and would qualify for many of the company prizes.

I was getting "Man of the Month" plaques quite frequently and some of my colleagues jokingly asked me to allow them to win one of the great prizes.

> *"Success is how high you bounce when you reach rock bottom."*
> —GENERAL GEORGE PATTON

Tragedy and More Disappointment

I really thought I was past my series of disappointments but I was now faced with a mammoth challenge. The Peugeot I bought started to overheat and was losing power. I took it to an expert who said the engine needed an overhaul. I tried to secure parts but my search was futile. Only one dealer existed in Jamaica and he stocked parts for the cars he repaired. My car was of French origin and I could not get the parts from the USA.

I was in a dilemma.

The government restricted the number of vehicles coming into the country and the available cars were expensive. I now had to travel on foot or use public transportation. I did not have the money to buy another car.

I felt like giving up as it seemed as if every time I found success in my life, obstacles would present themselves.

On the following Sunday morning, I attended church as usual but I was not motivated. I was seeing my dream die right in front of me. Despite my low feelings, I listened keenly to my pastor as he preached a sermon on faith. He said:

> Faith is the evidence of things hoped for and the evidence of things not seen". He went on to say, "If you want to be a victor you must first be a victim". "If you want to wear a crown you have to carry a cross". "If you want to reach the mountain you have to learn to deal with the valley.

I knew this message was the answer to my prayers and I knew the good Lord was speaking to me, urging me not to give up.

I now would take the bus from Brown's Town to St Ann's Bay. As the parish capital, St Ann's Bay attracted a lot of people. Many of the major offices were located there and people would stop to pay their utility bills as well. Based on these factors, I decided to use St Ann's Bay as my hub—a key decision for my future.

I also strategised down to the finer details such as how I would deal with my prospecting methods. I would now have to find places where I could spend the entire day prospecting and selling the company's products. These products were not as attractive as contemporary policies which offer investment facilities. Most of the policies available on the market in 1979 were whole life policies, ideal for persons who wanted to purchase insurance for the possible death or disability of the breadwinner. Many persons in the area did not know about Life of Jamaica as Mutual Life had dominated the landscape. One of their agents, Julius Dixon, was a household name in the area. I was having a real challenge as I now had to sell my company, myself and the products.

In St Ann's Bay, I travelled from office to office, introducing myself and offering my products. I heard the usual: *I have my policy with Mutual Life and I have an agent, I am not interested in anymore life insurance.*

I persisted, using all the training and experience I garnered to convince them why they should buy from my company. Slowly the tide began to turn. I began hearing that they had not seen their representative for years and they were dissatisfied with the service given. I promised to give them excellent service if they selected me as their agent.

I always believed that a picture is better than a thousand words so I gathered testimonials from clients who received good service from me. One powerful one, for example, would be written for me by persons for whom my company paid promptly on a death claim. This small act of gathering testimonials began to work in my favour. I was picking up two or three applications per day and I started to feel good again.

> **"Hope sees the invisible, feels the intangible and achieves the impossible."** —HELEN KELLER

A Strange Discovery

Back in 1971, I had a short stint working at the St Ann Parish Council. My brother was the Assistant Superintendent of Works and he secured a job for me as an Assistant Field Assistant. I had been driving by that office over the past year that I had been at Life of Jamaica. On one particular occasion I walked near the office and remembered that I had a friend there. I decided to call on him to say that I was now with a new company and was trying to procure new clients. He was happy to see me and said he had purchased insurance from Mutual Life but that I could still come to see him the next day.

I went back to see him and he bought insurance from me and also introduced several of his colleagues. I managed to sell a significant amount of insurance to people in that office for the month and later this became one of my main nests.

Further up the road from the Parish Council was the telephone company premises and there I discovered many technicians. They met at 7 a.m. for instructions to go in the field to work. I saw a gentleman I knew from my district and he introduced me to some of his colleagues. The following morning I was at the gate of the telephone company waiting for the men to arrive.

I made several appointments. In 1979, people who purchased up to $100 per month of life insurance could claim a part of the premium for tax reduction. Many had insurance with other companies but the service they were offered by their agents was inadequate.

I offered them my services and made sure to deliver on my promise. I sold insurance to several people, did income tax submissions for them and also filed all their taxes. As a result, they got a substantial return from the Income Tax Department, and of course they were very happy.

The news started to circulate around the office and all the other stations in St Ann. I began to sell a lot of insurance in these two areas and in three months I sold the most applications at my company. From this experience, I learned that having a car wasn't necessarily a vital asset. During the time I had the car I had passed all these places and did not stop to see anyone. Now while on foot, I was discovering my acre of diamonds.

My recent success allowed me to purchase parts for the car and overhaul the engine. I picked up my car from the mechanic in Kingston and returned to St Ann to continue the good fortune that I was enjoying.

On my way back, I reached the Bog Walk Gorge and learned that Flat Bridge was impassable. I would have to turn back and travel to Sligoville via Spanish Town. The car seemed to be running in great condition and I was taking it slow, following instructions from the expert. I was having good feelings as my branch manager expressed his delight that I was now the leading agent in the company and I was threatening to rewrite the company's sales records.

I had reached halfway over the high mountains in Sligoville, about to descend, when the car started to lose power.

It stopped in the middle of the road.

I had enough of this car. It was raining heavily so I could not get out to check what was wrong. A very kind gentleman stopped to enquire how I was doing and I asked him to secure the services of a wrecker truck on his way to Linstead. I sat in the car until the wrecker arrived. I told them I would return the following day to pay the bill. I had now decided to put away the car and would instead rent a car for three days each week. This worked out to be very good as I would work long hours during the days I had the car and sold a substantial amount of insurance to cover the expenses.

I was determined to achieve my goals at any cost.

> **"When you have come to the end of your rope, tie a knot."** —FRANKLIN D. ROOSEVELT

> **"When you have come to the end of the rope you have not come to the end of your hope."** —ANONYMOUS

A large portion of my business was now settling, and with "Projected Commission" I had a month of heavy earnings. I had been looking on the Ford Escorts that were coming out from the Northern Industrial Garage and I decided that I wanted to own one.

In the showroom was a beautiful yellow 1600 sport Escort with a black vinyl top and I learned it was for sale. I approached the owner, and made an offer that was less than his asking price and he accepted. I purchased the car for $9,500 cash. I decided then to deal with car problems permanently by owning three cars at all times to ensure that I could offset any possible issues. This would be a significant achievement as car ownership was a luxury in 1979. By the end of the year, I was going to surprise a lot of people.

CHAPTER 10
THE POLITICS OF CHANGE

BY JULY, JAMAICA WAS ABUZZ with political activity. The People's National Party was now in their second year of governance. From every walk of life, debates raged on about the future of our country.

The crime rate escalated to an unbearable level. Rumours that the government, led by "young Turks" in the party who were closely aligned to Cuba, were about to take the country into Communism.

This triggered a sense of fear amongst the people. Prospective clients stated that they were not going to buy any more insurance due to uncertainties about the country's future. Many contemplated migration. This was the result of *that* famous statement made by the great orator and prime minister of the day, Michael Manley. He basically threw out the challenge that there were five flights per day to Miami and those who did not like what he was doing should take one of those flights.

Many people took this statement seriously and anxiety abounded. Foreigners who owned villas in the St Ann area began to leave the island and put their properties up for sale. This caused an oversupply of real estate in the market and caused a ripple effect in the professional realm.

Several of my colleagues in the branch were preparing to depart but I had already made the firm decision that I would never leave Jamaica, irrespective of what opportunities awaited me overseas.

At this point, my friend Denzel Vaughn decided he would migrate to New York with his family. His manager tried to dissuade him as he felt Denzel had the ability to become the next president of the company. He could not get him to change his mind. I used this opportunity to increase my client list. I figured he would have some good clients at his disposal. I asked him for a few of his policyholders and this proved to be one of the greatest decisions I had ever made.

> *"A young man's hardest problem is to find a girl attractive enough to please him and dumb enough to marry him."* —ROBERT C. SAVAGE

My Great Discovery

I was now 26 years old and the thought of finding a life partner flashed across my mind frequently. I was so focused on my Christian commitment, and my insurance career, that there was little time left for me to think of anything or anyone else.

Despite having many prospects for the position of life partner, this was one area of my life that I did not want to make a mistake. I was not prepared to rush into a relationship.

I was waiting on the Lord's will for my life.

My friend Denzel, who by now was leaving, handed me a particular policyholder which was to be a parting gift. This person was from an area in Kingston with which I was unfamiliar: 36 Wright Crescent, Duhaney Park. The policyholder was Diana Henry.

Denzel lived in Duhaney Park for most of his life and was an elder at the Duhaney Park Assembly of God where the young lady worshipped. He was a close friend of her family and played a father figure role as her father had passed away some time ago.

I had no suspicions that Denzel had ulterior motives. I thought he had referred me to just another policyholder, but as they say, the rest is history.

I went out to find the address and drove around for thirty minutes without any success in finding the house. I thought of forgetting this one. I was not in dire need of clients and I estimated I could have sold three applications in that period of time.

I should have known that great discoveries can require several attempts.

This was proving to be divine destiny.

I eventually reached the house and saw a young lady sitting on the veranda. I introduced myself and said "I am the new insurance advisor who will handle your life insurance policy."

I had, until now, had only one intention and that was to try and sell her another policy. This would help me to win the company's top award.

I realised that she was very shy as she did not make eye contact with me for the entire time I spoke. Eventually, she looked in my eyes and I was struck by her pure beauty.

The Lord told me at that moment that *this was my wife.*

I then suspended the insurance interview and began to find out about who this proposed wife of mine was.

She was a humble, twenty-two year old who graduated from the University of West Indies with Honours in English, and was a teacher at the York Castle High School in my town of birth, Brown's Town.

She had returned to Kingston to pursue her postgraduate studies at the University. I must confess I had no problems in finding that address again. I invited her to visit my office for the rest of the summer holiday and help with the administration of my business.

She agreed.

I wanted her to understand the nature of my work. I was certain she would become my wife. She told me, "You are putting me to work without pay!"

I told her, she would get the return on her investment. I was now even more focused and determined to win. I had found a bright, beautiful young lady to share my life. Most importantly, she was a very serious Christian, exactly what I had asked the Lord for. She was the only daughter and was closely guarded by her mother who was also a school teacher. She did all her fact finding and I passed with flying colours. This was the start of what could be called a very short yet meaningful courtship.

Mission Accomplished

The end of 1979 approached and I was doing my best to hold onto the lead in the company. Many of my colleagues were planning to spring an upset but I was determined to be the number one man. The Company's books closed at the end of December and the final results were published.

I had now settled the most cases in the company and the most premium income. This meant I earned the most money as an agent.

I had topped all the key areas in the company and was appointed Chairman of the Production Club for the ensuing year.

1980 came and I was now the most popular agent in the company, and in just two years of employment. I was also able to go to the head office, and sit with all the officers of the company for the President's update on the plans and performance of the company's key sectors and its subsidiaries. This was very enlightening and became very useful when I entered management.

Invitations to speak came from many different places but I turned them down because I did not want share my secrets at that time.

I still wanted to hold the position for three years so I did not want to lose focus. In those days I did not speak much as I felt that should be reserved for people who liked that kind of exposure. My manager was an eloquent speaker and wanted me to be like him in this regard.

He arranged for me to do the Dale Carnegie Course in "Effective Speaking and Human Relationships". He paid for the course and I thought this was very generous. However, I considered turning down the offer as it was a three-month course that meant another trip to Kingston.

The course was very popular in Jamaica and was coordinated by the well-known motivator Clarence Denny. Most of the participants were managers and senior executives who had challenges with public speaking. I was uncomfortable in the initial stages. I had to do a lot of speaking in front of the class and I was still a very shy person.

I soon became a class favourite and I didn't miss a session. On the last sitting of the class which was graduation, we had to write a speech and present it on that day. I sat up the entire night to write my speech and delivered it to the best of my ability.

The class judged each presentation and selected the one most qualified as the best.

To my surprise, they voted for me as the best speaker.

I received a "Best Speech" pencil as my award, and I still have it today as a souvenir. It now seemed as if I had developed a way of becoming number one in everything I did.

> *"Dare to dream. Dream Big,*
> *but dream with your eyes wide open*
> *so as to see the opportunities that are emerging."*
> —ANONYMOUS

Opportunities Unbounded

It was early 1980 and people continued to depart Jamaica in droves for supposedly greener pastures in North America. Some individuals gave up lucrative jobs to work as domestic workers in the USA.

To get a visa to travel to the United States meant having to be at the Embassy from 5 p.m., the evening before! People devised ingenious ways to secure the most important commodity in Jamaica —a U.S. Visa.

Many insurance agents migrated. This led to a grand opportunity for me as policyholders were separated from their agents. I took on as many as I could and this was to be of significant benefit in years to come.

I did not lose sight of the dreams and goals I had when I started in 1978. I began thinking that it was wiser to purchase a villa, versus buying a house. No one wanted to buy resort properties. These properties were at giveaway prices on the North Coast. However, the financial institutions would not offer a long-term mortgage. I saw a three-bedroom villa in the Runaway Bay area listed for sale. The owner wanted to leave the island in a hurry and I managed to negotiate a good price without even knowing if a mortgage would be available. The asking price was $43,000. I was able to make an initial payment of $19,000 and now needed a mortgage to cover the outstanding amount. As I had suspected, no financial institution was willing to give me the mortgage even though I had the ability to pay.

Somehow, by divine intervention, I managed to secure a mortgage. My dream of buying a house by the sea had come true. With my first goal realised, I was ready to move on to goal number two—purchase my Mercedes Benz.

I went to my bank in Brown's Town and told the manager, "I need to purchase a Mercedes". He immediately told me about one that was for sale in Stony Hill, Kingston and the following day I drove to Kingston in search of the car.

I found it, inspected it, liked it and bought it instantly using my personal cheque. I drove it home, and just like that, dream number two was completed.

NEW MERCEDES BENZ AND VILLA BY THE SEA

When I returned to my hometown, many people were surprised. I now possessed three of the most expensive vehicles in Jamaica at the time. Some even whispered that I was dealing in the "green gold" in reference to marijuana, the growing of which was very popular in that part of the country. Soon after, the Jamaica *Daily Gleaner* chronicled my performance in the insurance business which effectively dispelled the rumour.

It was now April and the Company was celebrating ten years as a Jamaican entity. They celebrated with a convention at the Mallards Beach Hotel, now Sunset Jamaica Grande in Ocho Rios. It was a grand affair featuring a commemorative film about the company's history. The film also mentioned me.

The company lauded and awarded me for my record breaking feats for the previous year.

Danny Williams, the main speaker, gave a memorable presentation on how he started the company. He noted how he and his colleagues overcame obstacles and persevered when it seemed the company was going to fold. He went on to further speak about the topic of the day, the growing numbers of people who were migrating.

He predicted that if the People's National Party won the election, a mass exodus from Jamaica would result. However, if the Jamaica Labour Party won, the opposite would happen. This would prove to be a prophetic utterance. It did not go down well with the party of which he was an executive member and a close friend of Party Leader, Michael Manley. This appeared on the front page of *The Gleaner* in April 1980. My name also appeared with a caption identifying me as the number one agent in the company. This did a lot for my career at the time.

> *"Life is not measured by the number of breaths we take but by moments that take our breath away."* —GEORGE CARLIN

A Complete Awakening

Come June, and I prepared for what was to be an unforgettable experience. I had listened and read about the Million Dollar Round Table (MDRT) and my manager Tony Williamson was a regular attendee at the conventions. This was where all the top performers from around the world met each year to share ideas and listen to the best in the life insurance business.

The convention motivated people to achieve even higher levels of performance. Only six percent of all Life Insurance agents attended these meetings as there was a strict qualification standard.

That year we encountered some difficulty in acquiring foreign exchange. The government had enacted a statute that persons were only allowed to travel abroad with a total of US$50 per year.

I had a lot of money at that time but, as a Christian, I believed I should obey the laws of the land. I decided to travel to New York by faith with the allotted US$50. This would have to cover my hotel accommodation, food and the costs to attend the convention.

At the airport, I saw a colleague who worked at the Half Way Tree Branch. He asked, "Where are you staying in New York?"

"I don't know yet", I said. "I only have $50 but I'm travelling on faith."

"Well, my friend has a large house in Brooklyn, you can stay with me."

I was so happy for that offer, I accepted immediately.

On arrival, everything seemed fine and I retired to bed early as I was very tired. My friend woke me about 2 a.m. the following morning saying: "I made arrangements for you to go to a club my friend".

He even had a well-dressed, young lady for me, ready to party.

"No man", I said. "I am a Christian and not into that type of lifestyle."

He insisted but I refused and went back to sleep. The following morning he told me that I embarrassed him but by then I had already decided that I did not want to stay there anymore. I phoned a friend in Brooklyn and asked him to drive me to the convention which was scheduled to start that day.

I arrived at the convention, uncertain of my accommodations. I met some of my colleagues from the St Andrew Circle Branch, and they mentioned that our boss, Tony Williamson, had a Gold

ST. ANDREW CIRCLE STAFF AND THEIR SPOUSES CELEBRATE AT TRIDENT HOTEL AFTER WINNING FOOTBALL COMPETITION

American Express Card and had rented rooms for them at a Sheraton Hotel in Manhattan. I immediately contacted the boss and told him about my predicament. He made the arrangements for me to stay at the hotel.

God answered my prayer.

I was now ready for my MDRT experience.

The next few days changed my life professionally. I listened to some of the greatest speakers I had heard in my life. One of them, Ben Feldman, the most successful insurance salesman in the world at the time, was interviewed along with some of the greats on a panel discussion. He was asked why he was able to close all the sales interviews he conducted. He spoke in his own inimitable style:

> When you call a man over in Texas and tell him you are flying over to see him, don't you expect to see him under favourable circumstances? Do you expect him to say no when you ask him to buy?"

Ben Feldman had his own private jet. I now realized I was part of one of the greatest organizations in the world; the Million Dollar Round Table.

After my experiences at the convention, I was determined to put what I had learned, from the main platform and the closed sessions, to optimum use for my future development.

> *"Men and women chasing each other is what make the human race."* —MARK BELTAIRE

To Have and to Hold

After a year of wooing Diana, the great day of consummating our love affair was fast approaching. On July 12, 1980, I vowed to spend the rest of my life with my intended wife. The venue was set for the University Chapel in Mona, Kingston and the reception, at the Casa Monte Hotel in Stony Hill.

Pastor Clarke, my wife's pastor, and my own pastor, Rev. Everard Allen, conducted the ceremony. The master of ceremonies was the very funny Winston Bennett, the same man who had laughed at my dreams in 1978.

We had a wonderful day which continued on to our honeymoon at the Seawind Beach Hotel in Montego Bay. We then moved into our villa in Runaway Bay. This was a great achievement for me. I now lived in my own house, free from the burden of having to pay rent. While we lived in the villa, I observed tourists flooding the area. I had pledged earlier in the year, when I travelled to New York with just US$50 that I was going to set up a business to help to change the foreign exchange situation in Jamaica.

OUR WEDDING DAY, UNIVERSITY CHAPEL, KINGSTON

An idea came to me that I could rent the villa, earn some foreign currency and then buy a house for my wife and family. The villa was not appropriate for that purpose. I discussed it with my wife but she would have none of this idea.

It was our first disagreement.

Based on what was happening in Jamaica with people selling their properties and leaving the country, what she was saying sounded logical. I maintained my stance that I was going nowhere as I saw great opportunities for the future right here in Jamaica.

I had no money on hand but I had two of the finest cars available, parked in front of my villa. I was still indebted to the bank for these cars. I now had a wife and future children to take care of. I asked my bank manager whether he heard of any houses in the area being available for sale. A few days after, I got a call that someone had a house in Discovery Bay who really wanted to get rid of it. I contacted him right away and told him I was very interested in acquiring the property. The selling price was $33,000.

Of course I did not even have one dollar for a down payment.

It was now September; the political activities were in full swing with a lot of campaigning happening all over the island. Hand-in-hand with the political activities, the crime rate escalated with a frightening death toll. I even began to reconsider my stance to stay in Jamaica but I did not allow the situation to stop me from selling insurance.

The General Election was set for October 30 and both parties were confidently expressing that they would win. It was the Jamaica Labour Party however, that emerged as convincing victors. People celebrated in the streets. Danny Williams' prediction began to be realized as people started to filter back into the country.

I knew people who had sold their properties to migrate and came back to purchase those same properties, only to find the price of real estate had significantly increased.

I had managed to make a down payment of $3,300 for the house in Discovery Bay which became my place of residence, and has been for the past thirty-four years. The seller came to me saying that he had changed his mind, perhaps due to the changes in the political situation. He had now realized that the house was worth three times what he had it listed for.

I told him, "I am ready to close the deal. I have the cheque and we're ready to move into the house." Fortunately the deal closed and I was very happy that I had taken the risk to purchase. It was now time to reap the rewards.

Later that month, we moved to our new home in Discovery Bay. It seemed like my entire life progressed very rapidly. I was surprised about how much my life had changed, coming from basically nothing to achieving financial success. I now owned a Mercedes Benz, a sports car, a villa and my own house. Tremendous!

> *"Well done is better than well said."*
> —BENJAMIN FRANKLIN

The Dawn of a New Era

1980 had now come to an end and accordingly, the company results were published. Unfortunately, I was unable to hold on to the number one position in the company but I still settled the highest number of cases. I won the Danny Williams Trophy, qualified for the Million Dollar Round Table and was awarded the National Quality Award by the Life Underwriters Association of Jamaica. Despite having a very successful year, I was a little disappointed as I had planned to be the Chairman of the Production Club for at least three consecutive years.

The beginning of 1981 brought a breath of anticipation as there was a new government in power, headed by the visionary Edward Seaga. Many people who had fled the country continued to return to our shores and were acquiring real estate. The price of real estate was continuing to climb at a rapid pace and the people who had assumed the risk of staying in Jamaica started to receive a windfall.

Life of Jamaica, and indeed the insurance industry as a whole, had successfully waded through the turbulent seas of political uncertainty and was experiencing significant growth.

On the other hand, I had to deal with a great challenge. Several of my clients, who had left the island without my knowledge, could not make suitable arrangements to cover payment for their policies.

I had many lapsed policies to contend with. Fortunately, several of these clients returned to reinstate but this was not enough to get my performance levels to the required company standard.

I had reviewed the company's records and realised that no agent had ever settled over 300 cases in one year. I decided to surpass that record and aim for over 400 cases. I set out to accomplish what would be a remarkable achievement.

I had sat the Equity Linked Insurance Examination and passed. This policy was quickly gaining popularity in the field as the economy had started to experience inflation. People wanted to participate in investment as a means of mitigating the risks.

I worked out a strategy that would later yield great results. I wrote all my clients and informed them I was going to visit them soon with a great investment opportunity.

The company had a policy at the time called "Folio 5". This policy featured 50 percent of the premium linked with Jamaica Unit Trust facilities. I had personally purchased the policy and realized that the returns were great. I was now convinced that I would sell this policy to all of my clients. It would greatly assist them in securing their financial development.

By June, I managed to write a large number of Folio 5 policies. My manager was amazed at the amounts I had written and told me he wanted to visit me in St Ann to get a first-hand view of how I was closing that many cases. He came and worked with me for a week and

I am sure he was convinced that I was one of the best he had seen in regards to closing cases.

Those of us who have had the good fortune to work with Tony Williamson will know he would always have something up his sleeve. He said that the record for the highest number of cases written in any month was 75. He threw down his billfold on the ground and said "Strokey (as he called me in those days), if you give me a hundred cases in August, I will give you some cash." Despite seeing my ability, he still had some doubt that I could do it. I had so far written "only" 150 cases for the year.

I set out to work, and in August 1981 I wrote 181 cases and left my boss stunned. He was elated to say the least. He gave me the cheque and went to Miami to make a beautiful plaque with my feat inscribed. I have it displayed in front of me, in my study as a reminder, and I look on it every day. The news was now at the head office and as was customary in those days, a flyer with a successful agent's picture and accomplishments was circulated to all members of the company.

COMPANY FLYER ANNOUNCING
RECORD-BREAKING PERFORMANCE

I was a happy man.

Serious competition existed at Life of Jamaica as the agents had a great desire to be the Chairman of the Production Club. The managers also wanted to win the President's Trophy, their route to upward professional mobility. In our branch, other agents had begun to realize that they would have to step up their performance.

Tony had recruited a gentleman by the name of Godfrey McAllister, now Dr Godfrey. He was relentless in his pursuit to beat me at any cost but I was equal to the challenge. Tony sparked competitions between the agents and he threw his billfold on the ground even more frequently.

Godfrey generated a lot of cases but I still lead in all of the key areas that would allow me to be the top agent in the company. On occasions when he was under pressure, he went to St Ann to see if he could tap into some of the markets over which I had full control.

He did not succeed.

I had cemented my name in all the key places of employment in the parish. I offered impeccable service and most of my clients would alert me when other agents approached them to buy life insurance.

Fatherhood Beckons

My wife had now returned as a teacher of English at the York Castle High School. She was also pregnant. I was very happy that my first child would be arriving in the near future.

I had to now properly manage my time to ensure that Diana had my full attention and that I would still be able to take home the coveted top trophy from Life of Jamaica.

I was also now completing the final year of a two year Life Underwriter's Training Course and this added to what was already a full plate. August came and I patiently anticipated my child's birth.

I really was praying that it would be a boy.

I was a bit handicapped because my wife was going to give birth at the Nuttall Memorial Hospital in St Andrew. This deprived me of being in St Ann's Bay where I conducted most of my business.

On August 31st, my first child arrived, a beautiful girl who we named Patrice. The human side of me said, "I wanted a boy" but I quickly realised that God always work out His purpose for those who trust in him.

On that very day, I journeyed to St Ann to continue my quest for four hundred cases and purchased what was to become my favourite car, a 1977 Ford Escort Ghia.

I drove my daughter home from the hospital in that car and still have it today; in almost the same excellent condition I acquired it thirty-three years ago.

The end of 1981 was here, and the company results arrived.

During 1980, I had experienced a lot of lapses in the existing business portfolio which I had, and did not get an opportunity to reinstate the remaining cases. My conservation, the statistic that measures the percentage of business that remains in force after lapses, took a severe blow. It was now at 79 percent, below the company requirement of 89 percent which was needed to qualify for the award. I still managed to finish the year with 359 cases settled but this was below the number my main competitor achieved.

I however topped the company with premium income and first year commission. For another year I failed to become Chairman of the Production Club and was very disappointed. I was happy though as I was still the highest paid agent in the company.

CHAPTER 11
DETERMINED TO WIN

"Few cases of eye strain have been developed by looking on the bright side of things."
—RICHARD M. DEVOS

t was now 1982 and my colleagues and I attended our company retreat. I made a promise to all my colleagues that I would take my rightful position as the number one man in the company. Some of my colleagues said, "You're finished; you can't make it happen again." Obviously, they had not learned that when I set out to accomplish something, only God could stop me.

I made a pledge to make a clean sweep of all the major awards in the company. I also decided to upgrade to a new edition of my favourite car brand, the Mercedes Benz.

I sold the current one and began to search for a newer model that would fit my profile. I was not able to afford a jet to sail across the skies like the great Ben Feldman who had been an inspiration to me at the Million Dollar Round Table, but I was planning to buy one that would run on the ground. I wanted to earn all the money I could to purchase the car for cash in that year.

I had this goal along with the added change in my family situation. I now had a young wife and a beautiful daughter and I had no intention of sacrificing them for any success in the insurance business.

Time management was essential. I was fortunate to have an understanding and supportive wife. She did many of my assignments at home to ensure I had time to accomplish my goals.

I began the year as usual, blazing the trail with many applications written and settled. Again, my main competition was from the St Andrew Circle Branch in the form of the indomitable Godfrey McAllister. He was determined to take the top trophy again and was prepared to destroy my dream.

Other branches in the company were tired of our seeming domination and wanted their share of the pie. Accordingly, I soon realized that there was a dark horse in the race.

By the middle of the year, a gentleman from the Mandeville Branch, by the name of Anderson, had overtaken me. He had sent a message through his manager, the late Dickie Sampson that I should forget about the top award because there is no way I could beat him that year.

I was very happy and spurred by the competitive spirit that brewed. I now would have to draw up a new game plan.

I enjoyed the friendly rivalry that existed within the company and we would compete very hard; but it was always done in good spirit.

I happened to be passing through Mandeville in September and decided to check on my rival and threat for the coveted trophy. I walked into the Mandeville Branch and they greeted me warmly and ushered me in. I did not waste any time to ask to see Mr Anderson. I was taken to his office to meet him and without hesitation he told me to think of another year to win the trophy, as 1982 was his year. He had it covered. He proceeded to open the draw of his desk and pulled out a big bundle of applications which he had not submitted and said there were many more to come. I congratulated him on his fine performance and left on my way to Kingston.

> **"The big secret in life is that there is no secret; whatever your goal is you can get there if you are willing to work."** —OPRAH WINFREY

A Defining Moment

On my way to Kingston, a myriad of ideas ran through my mind about the type of strategy I would have to employ to give Anderson a knockout punch and silence him. I knew I was known in the company as one of the most prolific writers of cases and someone who was prepared to work long hours. I sat down and analysed the average number of cases I was writing and how much I would need to get ahead in earnings by the end of the record keeping in November. This would coincide with my birthday and would be a great present to myself.

I set out on my mission and was dogged in my approach. I almost closed everybody I interviewed. In October, I wrote in excess of 75 cases and wrote about the same amount in November. By the time the books closed, I was way ahead of my competitor.

I closed the calendar year in the same vein, writing and settling a lot of cases—with my competitor nowhere in the frame. I finally gave him that crucial knockout blow and I didn't hear much about him for my remaining years in the business.

The year came to an end and the results were now out.

I was declared winner of all the key trophies in the company as I promised earlier in the year. Of course I was thrilled. Mission accomplished!

I had now qualified for the Million Dollar Round Table for five consecutive years and only needed one more year to secure qualification as a Life Member. I thought this would be a phenomenal achievement. Only a few insurance professionals, across the world, had attained that qualification.

I made the decision that I wanted to win the top award for one more year and then focus on the managerial aspect of the business. In December, at our branch Christmas get-together, a gentleman who had recently joined our branch seemed to be inspired by my achievements. While all the celebration was going on, he pulled me aside and we went into my office on the ground floor. He told me he wanted me to tell him how I was able to operate at such a high level on a consistent basis.

I spent some time with him discussing particular ideas about how he could increase his productivity. He expressed great appreciation for the information he received. The name of this man was David Garel. I was not aware of his intentions to take me on in 1983 for the much sought-after top award. Nevertheless, I did not mind sharing my experience with him for such was the nature of the business. In my view, this is one of the few areas of business where people are willing to freely share their expertise with their colleagues.

My manager was at his fire starting best again, fuelling yet another competition. I now had another serious challenge in my branch and I was not prepared to yield. I set out to a get a clear lead, and I did.

This time around, the Montego Bay Branch, inspired by the levels of production I was achieving in St Ann, planned to do something about the sub-branch they had in Ocho Rios. The few agents they had were not making a good impression.

The pressure of operating from New Kingston was taking a toll on me as my portfolio of clients, who would have required my services, was increasing. I spoke to my manager about setting up my own office on Bravo Street in St Ann's Bay. I approached my good friend, Marjorie Taylor, who was the manager of the Jamaica National Building Society branch in St Ann's Bay about leasing the upper floor of her branch office.

I had developed a good rapport with her family, having taken care of their life insurance needs. She immediately agreed to give me a portion of the space for a minimum rental fee. I procured a sign and that essentially was the birth of the Ocho Rios branch which has contributed significantly to the company's performance and currently has been the top branch in the country for the past three years.

The news spread that a new Life of Jamaica office was now in operation in St Ann's Bay, and most people would pass the sub-branch in Ocho Rios and head to St Ann's Bay to conduct their business at my office. I employed a secretary and a messenger from my own resources.

I was now sitting in the office and clients would come in to buy life insurance. As I had promised myself, I now was able to buy a custom built Mercedes Benz and it definitely was beautiful. I bought it for $26,000 with my own personal cheque and I parked it in my garage under cover. I decided I would only drive it on special occasions as I had two other cars to take me to work.

IN MY OFFICE

In the coming months, sales of the Equity Linked policies continued to be a success for me as it was the most sought after product in the industry. Life of Jamaica, the leader in the life insurance market, sold a lot of these products and my clients loved the idea of having the best of both worlds. They benefitted from both the insurance and investment facilities which the product offered.

To my delight, one day I received a letter from the head of the Jamaica Unit Trust Fund, informing me that I was selected as the top producer of sales for the Equity Linked Insurance Competition and I should come to Kingston to attend an awards function where I would receive a Certificate of Merit and a cheque. I was very happy, especially about the substantial monetary award.

Coming from where I lost most of my opportunities because of lack of money, I was driven to make up for what I missed. I am reminded of a line in the movie, *Gone with the Wind*, which personally resonates with me. It's where Scarlett O'Hara, after the devastation of the Civil War, raises her hand to the heavens and declares, "As God is my witness, I will never be hungry again." Similarly, I declare what I want, I work hard at getting it and God manifests it for me.

> *"In between yesterday's regret and tomorrow's dream is today's opportunity. Seize the chance!"* —IFEANYI ENOCH ONUOHA

A Near Death Experience

On the morning of the awards, I got up to clean my Mercedes Benz for my trip into Kingston to receive my award. It was parked under cover for months and I had had very little time to take it for a ride. I had done some mechanical checks a few weeks before and I thought "There is no need to check it again. It has to be in perfect condition."

Assuming the car was fine proved to be a terrible mistake.

On my way to Kingston, I journeyed from Discovery Bay to Runaway Bay and the car seemed to be in the best of shape. When I reached the fishing beach in Salem, Runaway Bay, a white Toyota Corona, which was in front of me, came to a sudden stop as it approached a corner. I immediately applied my brakes but to my horror, the car proceeded at the same speed.

The brakes had failed.

The car was automatic and I could do nothing. My car spun out of control and ended up in the path of an Island Diaries' milk truck, coming at me from the opposite direction.

The truck hit my car at full speed and I knew this would be instant death.

I was rushed to the St Ann's Bay Hospital. I had lost consciousness but regained it at the hospital. By this time, news had circulated that I had an accident and died.

When I awoke, doctors surrounded me, including my client, the legendary Dr Buddy Wilson. He was the Chief Medical Officer and a beloved surgeon. The main building at the hospital is named in his honour.

Many of the hospital staff members were also my clients and I received the best of care.

To my relief, my only injury was a broken left arm. When I heard of the degree to which my vehicle was damaged, I was very grateful. I knew it was the Lord Himself who had intervened.

MY DAUGHTER STANDS IN FRONT OF MY RUINED MERCEDES, DAMAGED IN THE ACCIDENT.

After spending the night in hospital, I went home and couldn't recall ever feeling the level of pain I suffered. I was thankful the Lord had spared my life and I thought deeply about my wife and daughter.

My doctors advised me against doing any work for the next three months. It dawned on me then that my dreams were seemingly shattered.

It was the longest 90 days of my life.

After a few weeks of being at home, my mind fixated on the business of Life Insurance. I wasn't concerned about my income, so much, because I had weekly indemnity insurance paying my average weekly salary. I was concerned, however, about my clients and how they would manage with their policies. Subsequently, I hired a driver to take me around so I could continue to offer the same quality of service to them. This effort would ensure that the good year I was having would not end on a bad note.

Even though I was temporarily incapacitated, winning the top awards for 1983 was still on my mind. I wanted to get back into action.

I returned to work in the last quarter of 1983. I now had three months of production to catch up on in order to achieve my goals for the year. Unfortunately, even with three months of intensive selling, I came up short of the competition. The Chairmanship of the Production Club had slipped from my grasp yet again.

I was disappointed but after the year I had, I was just glad the good Lord had spared me to complete another year.

Beyond the Horizon

Although I did not win the top awards, two significant milestones were attained:

i. Qualification (for six consecutive years) for the Million Dollar Round Table (MDRT), an international, independent association that represents the world's best sales professionals in the life insurance industry. To qualify was a noteworthy achievement, as only a small percentage of insurance sales professionals worldwide qualified for Life Membership of this prestigious organization; and

ii. Qualification as Life Director of the Company's Production Club—a group consisting of top performing sales agents.

I had now qualified for every possible award at the company and felt I was only repeating them year after year. At this point, I thought of entering into the managerial aspect of the business.

Being in management would allow me to achieve the same levels of success I had attained in my career as an agent. I did not discuss this goal with my manager as I wanted to fulfil some other dreams: Of moving from Director to Chairman of the Production Club in that year. Afterwards, I would focus my energy on being the top Unit manager and top Branch Manager in the company.

In addition to my insurance career goals, I wanted to start a business to ease my chronic foreign exchange problem that virtually everyone in the country experienced. I was in the early stages of this plan and was about to acquire a commercial property on the main street in Salem, Runaway Bay. My initial intention was to start a car rental company and serve the growing tourist population in that area.

> **"If you will do the things today most others won't do, the time will come when you have the things most others cannot have."** —ZIG ZIGLAR

It was now 1984 and the insurance business was growing rapidly. Many new companies were being formed and many of the existing companies expanded. People were returning to the island to fill the employment positions in those companies and a few bright young professionals joined the industry.

I reflected on my six fantastic years in the industry and the prospects for the future looked good. My name was now a fixture associated with every company in St Ann and my competitors were starting to feel the pressure. Apparently, I made it difficult for some of the agents to find new business as I had secured the market.

At the company level, I set new sales records and raised the production standard of the company. The company was doing very well and had just secured a beautiful head office on Dominica Drive in New Kingston. This enabled the consolidation of the company's offices; formerly spread all over the city in rented and leased buildings.

The opening of the head office, officiated by Prime Minister, Edward Seaga, showed a sign of confidence because the country was experiencing far-reaching fiscal challenges and foreign exchange shortages. The resulting diminished purchasing power heavily impacted the company's efforts to market its products.

Inflation was also at a high level, contributing to the decrease of purchasing power, and this made people wary of putting their money in long-term savings and investments. Redundancies abounded in the public sector which also threatened to reduce our market for life insurance sales.

In spite of all the challenges facing the country, my mind focussed on one thing; to be the number one agent at Life of Jamaica. During that year, the company ventured into the group health insurance market and this created new opportunities for individual sales. Under the leadership of President, Adrian Foreman, the company also emphasised real estate as a long term investment in order to diffuse the effect of inflation. In 1984, real estate comprised 35 percent of the company's general fund investment. These assets included beautiful high-rise buildings in New Kingston which produced increasing values for the fund and a good image for the company.

As the year progressed, my sales increased and I had taken a lead role in every key area of the company's performance. In the spirit of friendly rivalry with my competitors, I told myself, "I would be unbeatable" that year. I had some great competition from a branch member who was close to surpassing me in sales. But, in the final two months of that year, I wrote a substantial amount of new business to stay ahead. I had also done my calculations and concluded that if I settled 75 percent of the business, no one could beat me for the top awards. I soon found out that someone at the head office, who was responsible for settling the business, had something else in mind.

> *"Envy is blind, and has no other quality but that of detracting from virtue."* —LIVY

An Unacceptable Situation

It was countdown time and I was not taking chances. My secretary checked all the applications to make sure they were clean and that all medicals and other underwriting requirements were provided. I delivered them to the office, by hand, to make sure they reached on time. Through systematic efforts like these, I had the best record for settling new business in the company. In November, I had cemented my position and was on the turn for the home stretch to claim all the top awards.

However, in December, I discovered that few settlements were coming through for me. A supervisor in the department assured me, "all clean business would be settled before the books closed on December 22". The day came and the company announced the results.

I was in second place, by the slimmest margin.

Something was utterly amiss.

My spirit had told me that someone did not want me to win, so I arranged a meeting with the Vice President and the Director of Marketing to find out what had happened. A thorough investigation was conducted and I received the upsetting news:

A young man in the underwriting department, who I supposedly had a good relation with, decided he was tired of seeing me win everything and concocted a scheme to give me some performance punishment. He hid all my applications so that they could not be settled and made sure every one of my competitor's applications was settled.

I expressed my outrage to his immediate manager and to senior management. The young man was reprimanded and transferred from that desk to another department. I received a letter of apology from the head office, and although they did not reverse the results, I was happy the young man would not have the opportunity to repeat his actions.

Despite the incident, the young man and I maintained a good relationship. Unfortunately in the ensuing years, he died. I was very saddened at his passing. I can only hope he had accepted the Lord as his saviour prior to his death.

At the end of the year, I had approximately 40 applications that should have been settled. Even though I was the number two agent in the company, I still had a good year because, technically, I was the top earning agent yet again. I also attained another significant milestone in my life. In August, my wife and I welcomed the birth of our second beautiful child, a son. We named him Andrew. Things were going well in my life.

Like icing on the cake, I received confirmations of my induction as an MDRT Life Member as well as Life Director of the company's Production Club.

CHAPTER 12
THE BEST IS YET TO COME

T WAS NOW 1985, and I decided I would not be competing for the top award as an agent anymore. I planned to service my clients, maintain my excellent record of high conservation and focus on going in to management. My manager did not think I was making the right decision as industry trends indicated that top producers did not make good managers.

I did my own research and the results were congruent with what he said but I wanted to break the mould. To accomplish this, I would have to do some studying. The company requirement for entering into management was to complete Part One of the Chartered Life Underwriter designation (C.L.U.). It would prove to be a challenging task, travelling to Kingston for the classes and staying up at night to study.

Despite my reservations, I attempted the course which had a total of three subjects. I failed, but it wasn't a big surprise—I did not put in the requisite amount of study.

Meanwhile, negotiations were taking place at the head office regarding the status of the Ocho Rios sub-branch. The Montego Bay Branch, located nearly two hours away, had started the sub-branch and wanted to continue to have responsibility for its management.

In order to see what was happening in the parish of St Ann, Michael Fraser, the company's vice president of marketing, visited both the St Ann's Bay office, for which I had responsibility and the sub-branch in Ocho Rios. While he was delighted with the St Ann's Bay operation, and even promised to refurbish my personal office, he was disappointed with the Ocho Rios sub-branch. I accompanied him to the sub-branch in Ocho Rios but when we arrived, the office was closed without any sign of activity. The company needed a presence in Ocho Rios and Mr Fraser pledged to rectify the situation.

I assumed word got to my manager, Tony Williamson, that there was an immediate need for a branch in Ocho Rios. He used the notion of my success in the parish to prove that his branch, St Andrew Circle, was best suited to oversee the development of the Ocho Rios operation. The mandate for its development was subsequently given to him. Our colleagues in Montego Bay were naturally not happy with this decision.

More changes were afoot. Tony Williamson had come up with a novel idea to build a "mega-branch" with 100 agents. As a result, he would need more managers. He conducted a survey, in the branch, to determine the best candidates for the transition to management. He did not release his findings but my intelligence in the branch told me I headed the list. Tony travelled all the way to my home in Discovery Bay, to tell me he was ready for me to join him in developing the 100-agent branch. He consequently began training me for a promotion to the position of Unit manager.

Sometime after this, I got a letter from the director of agencies asking me to move my St Ann's Bay office to Ocho Rios. He noted it would be impossible to build a branch in Ocho Rios if I was still facilitating clients in St Ann's Bay. This was a difficult decision to make, however, I was happy my clients would now have an adequate branch and receive maximum service.

1986 came and it brought a sense that I was edging closer to my desire to reach the next level. The Montego Bay Branch had found it difficult to recruit new agents for the Ocho Rios sub-branch from that distance, so it did not grow. It was now the job of St Andrew Circle. Even though it was difficult to find quality agents in Ocho Rios, I managed to recruit several agents within six months. We held an event and rebranded the sub-branch as part of St Andrew Circle.

A Childhood Dream Realised

By this time, the urge to diversify and start my own business re-emerged. I approached my bank to start a car rental company on the commercial property I had acquired in 1983. The bank manager required a projected cash flow plus one third of the initial capital outlay for the business. New motor cars were difficult to acquire and I would have to get used cars to start the business. His assistant was my past school colleague, so I requested an old cash flow template so I could do it myself – instead of paying an accountant the $2,000 it would have required.

I stayed up all night and prepared the Cash Flow Statement and other documents requested by the manager, but I didn't have the required cash. The manager commended me for the Cash Flow Statement but he could not give me the loan without the required equity in cash.

I hit on a plan to raise the cash. When I was a youngster, I used to repair cars, read auto magazines, and hang around the garage where they prepared cars to race at Vernam Field in Clarendon. I believed this skill would now come in handy. I knew of a garage that was selling its equipment so I decided to repair cars and raise the capital to purchase it. The bank manager instructed his assistant to open a current account with a $6,000 overdraft. I had already incorporated a company with the name Salem Motors Company Limited so I was ready. I started the business with 100 percent capital from the bank by quickly securing two contracts from companies to repair vehicles in their fleets. I also hired some of the finest repairmen and purchased good equipment which helped me to build a reputation for quality repairs.

Within the first year, I earned a significant sum and had achieved a profit. Since I was now ready to earn foreign currency, and I needed three cars to commence formal operations, I reapplied for the bank loan. Again, he rejected my application because the money the business had made was insufficient to purchase the cars. However, he was impressed with the company's performance and would see what he could do. These were the days when bank managers would visit your premises and give advice as well as aid in securing what was needed to make your business successful.

Armed with my own desire to increase my financial status, I was determined to achieve success with the business to help to solve the country's foreign exchange problems.

Meanwhile, certain structures had to be put in place so that the business could succeed. My wife had now switched from teaching at York Castle High School to St Hilda's Diocesan High where she was doing an excellent job teaching English Language. At home, we had now secured the services of a full-time helper to care for our children. It wasn't long before we realized this arrangement was not working out.

We made the decision that my wife would stop teaching, and take care of the children as well as oversee our new, rapidly expanding business. She was elated to be able to spend quality time with our two children. This would prove to be one of the best decisions we ever made. Since there would be a shortfall in income, due to my wife's new role, I knew I would have to fill the gap to compensate for this change.

> *"All your dreams can come true if you have the courage to pursue them."* —WALT DISNEY

A New Dispensation

The news was now out; I was appointed a Unit manager. I was never told that I could not succeed in management but the vibes I got suggested I would not make the grade. It has been said that top salesmen would make poor managers and research upholds that claim, but I was not daunted. I actually relished the challenge as my life had been a constant story of people doubting my capability. As the saying goes, "The greater the possibility to fail is the greater the opportunity to succeed" so I wanted this to be my reality. I was prepared to silence the naysayers as I did before as a salesman.

Over the years, I had observed a high turnover of agents in the business, so I concluded the reason for this to be poor recruiting methods. I could not say this was true of my branch as we had produced the top agent in the company for six consecutive years. Tony Williamson had an adage that he would use with his managers quite often, "You can't make ice cream out of putty; we have to get milk." In other words, if you want to get high level production, you needed to recruit quality agents. I was determined to be the number one unit manager in the company, and the secret weapon I would use would be quality recruiting.

It was now 1987, and I was still committed to ensuring that my car-rental business would get off the ground. One morning, on my way to the Ocho Rios office, I got a message from my bank manager to see him immediately. I turned my car around and went back to St Ann's Bay to meet with him. The bank had a motor car for sale and he was offering me a loan to purchase the car. I would have to make a 40 percent deposit but I did not have the money. I was now experiencing a cut in income, one of the expected initial experiences of sales management. With less time to focus on your own sales, income from this source falls. Meanwhile, it would take some time for the returns from my investment in building my unit to bring my earnings to a level close to what I earned during my agent status. I brazenly told him I wanted a 100 percent loan, and he laughed.

After I sat with him for some time negotiating, I received the full purchase price as a loan to purchase the bank-repossessed Toyota Corolla.

Salem Car Rental was born.

I had started the business with zero capital. I now realized I had to be astute in the management of my time so I could successfully manage both ventures. I had never worked on Sundays since I came into the insurance business, and was always at church for two services on Sundays. But I now had a business to manage, a large portfolio of clients to service and no room for compromise on the latter as I had given my clients my word.

In order to realize my dream of becoming the top unit manager in the company, I had to recruit top level agents. I also had a young wife and two precious children to look after so I was determined to achieve maximum success in every area of my life. With faith in the Lord, I knew I had succeeded already. But somebody once said "Not even the Bible promises a loaf to the loafers." I knew I had to play my part in putting in some serious work.

Many things were happening all at the same time. We had to move to larger office space on Newlin Street to accommodate the new agents I had recruited. Meanwhile, I was back on the street, selling insurance, where I had started my career. While I was thus preoccupied, news came from the office that blindsided me: A manager was appointed for the soon-to-be branch—without my knowledge.

I was devastated, not because I wasn't selected as manager. It was due to the fact I had sacrificed a year of my income and skill to develop the sub-branch and I wasn't even informed of the managerial appointment.

When the news circulated in Ocho Rios, many of my competitors called, saying: "You got a bad deal, now move on". The Lord spoke to me, however, telling me not to resign, support the new manager and continue working as hard. Also, I should wait for the day when I would be in charge, promotion comes from Him alone.

The incident infused within me a drive to show them the real me. I was still focused on building the best branch in Life of Jamaica and I knew my input would be vital. It was clear to me; I had the connections, skill and social status in the area to make the branch thrive.

> **"There is only one way to succeed in anything and that is to give everything."**—VINCE LOMBARDI

The Defining Moment

By the year 1988, we had recruited new agents and again required more space. I was given the charge to locate a property that the company could buy. Life of Jamaica had acquired the Jamaica Citizens Bank some years before and was planning to open a branch in Ocho Rios. I quickly identified an ideal location for the Life of Jamaica office as well as the bank, but a good friend had already made a down payment on the property. I told him what the company was looking for and he agreed to put in the infrastructure for the bank. Life of Jamaica rented most of the building, from which the branch still operates today. The company subsequently opened a branch of the Jamaica Citizen's Bank on the lower floor of the building.

I had enrolled in the Agency Management Training Course (AMTC), gaining insight in directing the selection and retention of agents. This would become a valuable asset in my quest to become the top Unit manager in the company. We had now reached the minimum number of agents required to start a branch. My unit performed reasonably well but I needed to recruit top level agents in order to compete with the agents in Kingston. It was quite difficult to attract top level agents in the area as most of the more competent persons had migrated to Kingston, and the rest were very comfortable in their present employment. I started to recruit individuals in the age group of 35-45. I felt these persons exhibited a greater sense of stability and would be able to attract the quality of business that would help our unit prosper.

Our branch manager, Kemorine Miller, was the first woman in the history of the company to be appointed as branch manager. She wanted to put her name in the annals of the company's history as the first woman to win the President's Trophy, the most sought after trophy in the company. Under her management, the unit performed reasonably well but I was not pleased. It was difficult to perform at our optimum best as we had to move offices and we spent a lot of time setting up the new branch. However, we now had a beautiful office environment, with everything we needed. It was time to deliver.

> *"Security is mostly a superstition. It does not exist in nature, nor do the children of men as a whole experience it. Avoiding danger is no safer in the long run than outright exposure. Life is either a daring adventure, or nothing."* —HELEN KELLER

We had been enjoying good weather and the hurricane season had been quiet thus far. I had heard many stories, in my lifetime, about the storms that had passed through Jamaica over the years. On one morning in September 1988, I awoke to strong winds and rain. Since the zinc shed covering my cars could easily collapse, I moved all the cars from my business place in Runaway Bay and parked them at the back of my house. I checked on my villa in Runaway Bay and was on my way back home when Hurricane Gilbert struck.

On reaching Pear Tree River, the water from the sea was coming across the road and I had to quickly accelerate to avoid being marooned. It was a frightening experience which multiplied when I entered my house and the full brunt of the storm struck. The entire country was on lock-down, everywhere in darkness.

Electricity did not return for three months. Due to the terrible storm, the year ended with all the targets I had set out to achieve being shattered, but I was grateful to the Lord when I considered the many who had lost their lives and the properties that were completely demolished.

A Desire to Win Again

One of my favourite motivators is the late Zig Ziglar, author of my favourite book, *"See You at the Top"*. The book mentions Proverbs 27:20 which presents a fact that is undeniable on the human level. "Just as death and destruction are never satisfied, so human desire is never satisfied." Maslow in his Theory of Motivation, stated:

> Man is a wanting animal and rarely reaches a state of complete satisfaction except for a short time. It is the characteristic of the human being throughout his lifetime that he practically always desires something.

As a Christian, I believe that those whose eyes are ever towards the Lord, in Him are satisfied and shall ever be so. Ziglar asked the question, "How do people get what they want?" Here is his key to unlock this mystery:

> You can have everything in life you want if you will help enough other people to get what they want.

My ultimate aim therefore, would be to influence and motivate my young unit and the new agents I was going to recruit. This would help them to achieve what they wanted and to help me to attain an extraordinary achievement of being the number one Unit manager in the company.

It was time to step up my efforts to win the Unit Manager trophy that year. The rumour circulated that I could not make it as a manager. I was planning to get so good at management that I would be able to run my own branch. I had gotten my production quota, and it was a reasonable one. I had also shared my vision with the members of my unit and told them what was in it for them. I again realised the need for a true top level, super-agent like myself so I recruited a young lady, Mavis Ferguson, who I had met at the Marcus Garvey Secondary School. She was hungry for success and wanted a career opportunity. I believed she was a perfect fit for my super-agent team.

I then realised that agents recruited in the current year, 1989, would not be counted in my quota, and that the secret would be to include as many agents as possible in the ensuing year. This would lead to a large percentage over the quota, which was a key element in winning the trophy.

While I was planning my way to the coveted trophy, I learned that a gentleman by the name of Derrick Bernard, with whom I had a good relationship, had the same goal. I heard through the grapevine that he wanted to open his own branch in Montego Bay, and winning the Unit Manager's Trophy would put him in an excellent position to cement his dream. He started off the year way out in front and kept on moving ahead. He was in "win or die mode".

During September, the agents had their annual Production Club motivational seminar at the Jamaica Grande Hotel in Ocho Rios. They gave me a citation and honoured me for being one of the top 25 agents in the history of the company to be appointed as Senior Life Underwriter. To qualify for this designation required ten years of continuous high levels of production and a minimum average of 89 percent conservation of business. I had just completed ten years with the company and felt proud of my achievement. I was motivated to press on to complete my goal for 1989.

By this time, our beloved Danny Williams was back in reign as president of the company. It was customary to hold a managers' retreat in the last quarter of each year. These retreats were designed to motivate managers so that the company quotas would be met. Our president gave a great motivational talk and instilled in us a lot of hope for the future.

> *"The difference between the impossible and the possible lies in a person's determination."* —TOMMY LASORDA

A Very Embarrassing Moment

During the retreat, Derrick Bernard, my competitor, sought and got permission from the chairman of the retreat, Michael Fraser, to make an address. He announced that it was fruitless for the Unit managers to consider competing for the trophy that year as he could not be defeated. He had a special word for me, the next man in line to win the trophy.

He made fun of me.

He also boasted about what he would do when he reached the Promised Land. I was very embarrassed but I did not say much. I told myself that I would do whatever I could to silence him.

In working out my game plan, I realised I would have to do some of the selling myself and it would take a team effort to make this plan succeed. I had several new agents whose contract began on the first of October; one of them was Mavis Ferguson. She had demonstrated great skills in writing a large number of applications. Fortunately, all my agents caught the vision and they were working hard to bring it to reality.

> *"We are what we repeatedly do; excellence therefore is not an act but a habit."*
> —ARISTOTLE

I was now monitoring the settlement levels of both units weekly and unfortunately we were not closing my competitor's lead. Something drastic had to be done.

In October, I had a client, who was a good friend, reveal that he was about to start a large business venture and needed a significant sum of money to borrow—approximately six million dollars. The bank informed him, he would have to purchase life insurance for an amount equivalent to the sum he was borrowing. To my surprise, several sales representatives had already given him proposals for life insurance, but he told me he was not prepared to buy the policy. He noted that it would have been too much money for him to pay along with the monthly interest payments that the loan would attract.

I saw the need to act quickly as there were four other agents who were pursuing what was to be the largest insurance policy written at Life of Jamaica.

I returned to my office to prepare my own proposal. One policy I offered him was a "Term Life" policy, with investment features and a premium of $125,000 per annum. He also got another proposal from my company, a "Folio 4" policy, a permanent insurance policy linked to a real estate investment fund, and this had a premium of $250,000 per year. He was constantly mentioning the high premiums that he would have to pay so I tried to convince him to take the "Term Life" policy. However, he was not prepared to buy any life insurance, and, if the bank was not willing to lend him the money without the insurance, he would scrap the project. I knew I had to do something extraordinary if I wanted to provide a solution to my client as well as further my own goals.

The end of the year was fast approaching.

> *"Good instincts usually tell you what to do long before your head has figured it out."* —MICHAEL BURKE

While pondering on my dilemma, I remembered one of the speakers at the Million Dollar Round Table Convention shared how he dealt with a case similar to mine. He said, he had gone to sell insurance to a businessman, who needed to secure a loan, but the businessman objected because he thought that the bank was playing hardball. He asked a simple question that the prospect could not answer and that was the breaking point which made the businessman sign the life insurance application.

I was ready to try anything to close the case, to satisfy my client's needs as well as my own. I pictured myself and my unit sitting at the Pegasus Hotel with great pride, receiving the trophy. I proceeded to ask my client, "If it was your money in the bank, would you like the bank to lend it to the customers without proper security?" To my great surprise, I got a big smile from him. He did not answer the question and neither did I solicit an answer. He told me he would think about it and call me if he changed his mind.

Meanwhile, my agents were submitting a lot of applications and our position was improving but we needed to do something immense.

The week following the interview with my client, I stood at the entrance to my office and heard someone calling my name. I turned around and saw my client. He hastily said I should come up to his place of business and sped off in his car. A great feeling started to overtake me and I rushed to my office to prepare myself for what was to come.

Not long after I was at his office. He went in his desk drawer and gave me the greatest shock in my life insurance career. He pulled out about six proposals he had received, and selected one. He said he was not interested in the proposal I had given him for the "Term Life" policy as he wanted to purchase the "Folio 4" policy.

My response to his objection had apparently done the trick. Thank the Lord! What a moment.

I swiftly completed the application and walked out of his office on cloud nine. However, as had been the story of my life, my challenges were far from over.

Creating History Out of Defeat

I submitted his application to the head office and hoped my client would pass the required medical examination. I drove him to the Oxford Medical Centre in Kingston for the medical which took the entire day.

> *"It's not enough that we do our best; sometimes, we must do what is required."*
> —WINSTON CHURCHILL

All the requirements were now fulfilled for the case to be settled but I wasn't getting any feedback from the underwriting department in head office. It was now December, and I had little time to spare, so I made an enquiry at the head office to ascertain what was happening. Unfortunately, I got some bad news.

They were about to decline the application as the medical indicated that my client had a heart condition.

My client was surprised as he recently had a check-up and was not aware of the heart condition. He contacted his personal physician to discuss the matter and also called the company's Underwriting Department to have further dialogue. Additional tests were done and thankfully the man had a clean bill of health. I was now happy that all the hurdles had been seemingly surmounted. All I needed to do was collect the initial premium payment to close the deal. However, I could not collect the initial premium from the client because the company could not find a reinsurer anywhere in the world to underwrite such a large policy.

The deal was still up in the air.

I must confess, I got very angry and directed some of my frustration at the Underwriting Department. I did my own investigation and found out that there were some people in the department who were not keen on getting the policy settled. Yet another person thought this little country boy was achieving too much. The memory of a similar incident in 1984 was fresh in my mind, but this time around I was taking hold of my dream and nobody could deny me the opportunity of achieving it.

I went upstairs to see the Vice President in charge of Marketing, Michael Fraser, and explained my feelings about the case. He then contacted Hillary Jardine who was in charge of the New Business Department. A meeting was then convened to discuss the matter. I told them that I didn't know how they were going to do it but I had no intention of telling the applicant that we could not place his application, after all the problems we had put him through. I headed to Ocho Rios. This was the 20th of December, 1989, just two days before the books closed.

I updated the members of my unit about what was taking place and they were all praying that things would work out in our favour.

The following morning I got up very early and went to my office to await the call; to find out if they found a reinsurer, and to get the green light to collect the initial premium. The call did not come until the following morning. Yes, they had found a reinsurer in Germany to take the case. I collected payment from the client and drove to Kingston to ensure that it was paid at the head office. I wanted no excuses for non-settlement of the case.

In the final hours before the company closed its books for 1989, my competitor, Derrick Bernard was still the leading Unit manager. It didn't seem likely that I would unseat him. I had acquired a cellular phone, a relatively new technology at the time, and I was among the first set of persons in St Ann to own one. I had asked someone in the

New Business Department to call me when the policy was settled. I was on my way to St Ann, from Kingston, and when I reached Mt. Rosser, my phone rang.

The application was settled.

Elated, I could not wait to share the news with my unit.

We celebrated all afternoon. It was revealed to me that the highest premium ever associated with a policy sold by the company, was $75,000 per year and the company's computer programme could only compute a $100,000 premium.

I had broken yet another record at Life of Jamaica. Glory to God! What a feeling!

The company had to create a new computer programme to facilitate this and other applications that would exceed the previous threshold.

I did not hear from my good friend Derrick Bernard for several months and he did not attend the Company's Award Function to watch me accept my trophy. I would have liked to share the moment with him. In December of 1989, the company experienced the highest amount of sales in any individual month in the history of the company and my unit had made a tremendous contribution. We did in excess of 1000 percent of our quota in that month.

> **"Some people stand on the promises; others just sit on the premises."**—ANONYMOUS

The 1990s had arrived and Life of Jamaica was entering its third decade of existence. Under the control of the newly formed ICWI Group of Companies which had Dennis Lalor as its chairman, the company was seeking to become a global institution while looking for opportunities to earn foreign exchange. The first of such opportunities occurred when Life of Jamaica entered an agreement to acquire Caribbean Atlantic's portfolio of Manufacturer's Life Financial Services. The ICWI Group welcomed the challenges as it held the ambition of becoming a Fortune 500 company. I was determined to share in the company's success and happy to work for such a progressive organisation. I set my plan for 1990, and told my unit that we must win the Unit manager's Trophy at least two times to prove that we are really champions. Anything less and we would be deemed to have been just a 'flash in the pan'.

The insurance industry was booming, and many banks and other financial institutions were eager to move into this lucrative market. The Eagle Group of Companies decided that they wanted to get a better share of the market and were in search of an insurance guru who could help them to achieve that goal. They really had nowhere to look but to Life of Jamaica as we had the best leaders and managers in the industry. They made the indomitable Tony Williamson an offer which was hard to refuse and he accepted it to become the President of Crown Eagle Life Insurance Company. This had an impact on my branch in Ocho Rios, as one of his recruits and close associate, Kemorine Miller, also my branch manager, was drafted to become the Vice President of Marketing at Crown Eagle.

I also got my own offer. Earlier in the year, a gentleman by the name of Pat Swaby was sent by Island Life to Ocho Rios to build their Ocho Rios sub-branch. He spent some time in the area trying to recruit new agents and to build the outfit. But he found it difficult. I got a call from him one morning and he invited me to meet with him. He was impressed with my work in the area and he wanted to recruit me. I did not even think about it. I declined immediately. I had no thought whatsoever of going anywhere. My spirit told me that the best was left to come and I should stand firm.

On the fifteenth of June, my wife gave birth to our third child, another beautiful baby boy whom we named Kirk. I felt happy that he was delivered safely and that my wife was in good health. I now had three children to take care of. This was not a problem as all plans were in place to see them through to university.

Mid-July of 1990, and the impending move of our manager was affecting the smooth running of the branch. The agents did now know who would be their next leader. They invited me to a meeting one morning to try to find out who would succeed the outgoing manager but I could not give a definitive answer as I was not informed by anyone.

Since the outgoing manager had to make preparations for her new assignment, she could not effectively deal with the affairs of the branch. I volunteered to assume this responsibility as I did not want to have to start a new branch when my opportunity for management presented itself. At the same time, I could not envisage the company sending someone else to head the team after all the work I had done in the community, coupled with my proven ability to build and create new opportunities. I was concerned though when I did not hear any word from senior management.

To end the uncertainty, I arranged to meet with the vice president, at his office in Kingston, to discuss the concerns of our team. He advised me that the company was having a challenge in filling the position. I, in reply, asked him in a forthright manner: "Am I not being considered for the position?" From his response, I gleaned that other branch managers were opposed to my potential appointment. Apparently, I did not have the requisite experience and there were many others before me who were waiting on the opportunity for promotion. I really could not believe what I was hearing and I decided to press him hard. I had to remind him of my contribution towards the development of the branch, and he must have seen I was having none of what he was saying.

I left his office, very upset.

I continued to conduct branch meetings, to keep the morale high, as I was sure that someone with wisdom would come to the realization that I was the man for the job.

A few weeks elapsed and I got a call from the head office that the president, Danny Williams, wanted to see me at his office on the following Tuesday evening at 2 p.m. I did not know the nature of our meeting but I must confess I was a bit nervous. Knowing the nature of the person I was going to meet made me feel a little relaxed.

I had many conversations with Danny over the years, including one particular instance in 1989 at the Manager's Retreat in Ocho Rios. I had sat at his table for lunch and he asked me how my car rental business was doing. I was shocked as I was not aware he knew about my secondary business. I quickly responded that I was having problems with the loan I secured from the bank. He gave me some sound financial advice and recommendations, one of which I considered very seriously and still follow today.

He advised me not to procure any more loans as I had the ability to sell enough insurance to purchase all the cars I needed. I shouldn't be wary of putting all the cash I had in the business. He also shared with me some of the things he had to do to get Life of Jamaica off the ground.

I followed his advice, and today Salem Car Rental is a great success story.

With those good memories, I decided to calm my nerves. I reached his office approximately 1:50 p.m. His secretary announced my arrival, and to my surprise he stepped outside his office and invited me in. As I entered through the door, I saw that my good friend and Executive Vice President, Herbie Hall was already meeting with Danny. Surprisingly, he asked Herbie to give him 15 minutes as he had to speak with me. He offered me coffee and made sure I was relaxed. At this moment, my spirit told me I was onto something good.

He first apologized for the pain and rejection I must have felt over the past weeks. He was off the island when the position became available and when he heard of it he summoned me. He congratulated me on the outstanding work I had done in the branch and for the company. In a nutshell, I was the best man for the job. He reiterated his confidence in my ability to take the Ocho Rios branch to the number one position in the company.

Well, what I can say is that I promised him when that moment arrived I would invite him to speak at my Annual Awards Breakfast.

What transpired in that office has led to an indelible impression on me of the man. When you walk into my office the first thing that will hit you is a portrait of Danny. I am not surprised that this man is one of the most respected humanitarians and businessmen in Jamaica today.

Armed with the confidence he expressed in me, I had only one option.

Deliver!

CHAPTER 13
MAKING HISTORY IN THE INSURANCE INDUSTRY

"There has never been a statue erected to the memory of someone who let well enough alone." —JULES ELLINGER

IN **OCTOBER 1990,** I was appointed Branch Manager, Ocho Rios branch. I was amazed by the congratulatory letters and calls I received from within and outside the company. Even my competitors expressed delight about the news of my appointment.

I was not only experiencing upward mobility in my job but my business was growing rapidly as well. My wife was now involved full time and my dream in 1979 of earning foreign exchange was now a reality. I had done my usual research and discovered that no member of the sales team had ever topped the three main sections of sales related areas, i.e. Top Agent, Top Unit Manager and Top Branch Manager. This was now one more record I could create, and

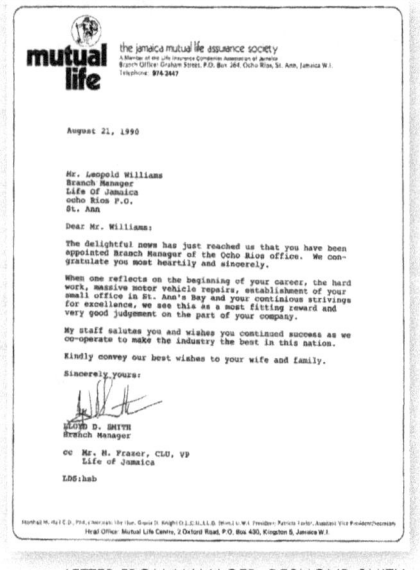

LETTER FROM MANAGER, DESMOND SMITH, MUTUAL LIFE INSURANCE COMPANY

nothing or no one but the Lord could stop me from achieving my goal; perhaps not in this already challenging year for the Branch, but certainly in the short term.

My first plan was to send a letter to the 15 agents in the branch informing them of my new appointment. Many of these agents were already receptive to my leadership because I had recruited them.

At the end of 1990, the branch finished 14th of the 15 branches in the company. I vowed this would never be the case again as long as I was the team leader.

> **"Management is doing things right;
> Leadership is doing the right things."**—PETER DRUCKER

During this time, the company conducted a survey to measure their impact in each parish in respect to market penetration. At one of our company retreats, when the figure came up for St Ann I was given commendation for the growth of the company in the period I operated there. The Company decided that they would separate the non-corporate area branches and place them under the supervision of John Haughton, a newly-appointed Director of Agencies. This proved a successful marketing strategy as there was intense competition between the corporate and the non-corporate branches, yielding increased production for the company.

Come 1991, my main objective, as stated at our retreat in January was to increase the manpower of the branch. In addition, I was pleased with the commitment I got from my team with regard to what they were prepared to accomplish in the ensuing year. It would be a challenge, but we could do it.

The company, now in its twenty-first year, had come of age. A big celebration was planned, resulting in many articles circulating in the print and electronic media. Several functions were held and a big awards event was to cap the celebration.

At this event, I glowed in the spotlight, accepting three beautiful plaques for my contribution to the development of the company. One was for my ability to write large numbers of cases, another was for being Chairman of the Production Club twice, and the other, for attaining the distinction of being appointed a Senior Life Underwriter. These awards motivated me to a new level. I was, more than ever, determined to transfer this excellence to the area of management.

ACCEPTING AWARD FROM LIFE OF JAMAICA PRESIDENT R. DANNY WILLIAMS, FOR OUTSTANDING CONTRIBUTION TO THE SUCCESS OF LIFE OF JAMAICA

As the year progressed, the branch moved up in the company's standings and we saw some stars in the branch starting to shine bright. One of those agents was Mavis Ferguson. I had coached her to qualify for the Million Dollar Round Table (MDRT) in the first three months of her contract. I had promised Mavis that if she sold enough business to qualify for the MDRT, I would take her with me to the MDRT Conference in Chicago and buy her lunch. She took my proposition seriously and she wrote a large number of applications. We had a wonderful time at the Conference. She is currently the manager of the Ocho Rios branch of Sagicor Life Jamaica (formerly Life of Jamaica), and has been the leading Branch Manager for the past three years; a success story indeed.

The year ended with some measure of success but I knew it would have been difficult for us to take home the top awards. Nonetheless, we focused on getting the manpower numbers to a reasonable level, moving from 12 to 20 agents and increased the conservation rate from an unacceptable 78 percent, to above 90 and were able to win the trophy for being the Top Non-Corporate Branch. We were featured in the company's Life's Like This magazine and one of my agents, Joline Whiteman, placed third overall in the Employee Benefits Trophy. Our standing in the company improved, assuring the branch's future. I also earned the Master Branch Award from the Life Insurance Managers and General Agents Association for an excellent record of high level agent production and effective middle management development. Several calls and letters of commendation from the head office came in for the quick turnaround in performance of the branch.

> **"Be willing to make decisions. That is the most important quality of a good leader."** —T. BOONE PICKENS

During this period, I appointed two new unit managers. By so doing, these middle managers would have an opportunity to contribute to the growth of the branch by recruiting and developing agents, while achieving their own desires for upward mobility.

> **"It is right to be content with what you have, never with what you are."**

It was now 1992 and we had our Annual Retreat and all emphasis was being placed on winning the President's Trophy. I really wanted to win this time around and I just could not wait anymore. The non-corporate branches met, and the feeling was the same among us. Director of Agencies, John Haughton, gave us some history of branches that had won the coveted trophy over the years and said "no branch outside of Kingston had won in the last fifteen years". He wanted one of our branches to take home the trophy.

I was now even more excited as I liked to do what others failed to achieve. I was always looking to break records and was so proud to lead the number one non-corporate area branch in the company. My good friend Tony Tomlinson in Mandeville, however, felt a little jealous and warned me, "I'm coming to get you." I addressed the group and responded: "It won't be easy!" This was the type of competitive camaraderie we thrived on.

During the year, we travelled to Texas together for the LAMP Management Conference (Leadership and Management Programme), and had a wonderful time, but when we got back it was serious competition.

Mandeville took an early lead and was on fire. We tried hard to increase production in the branch but could not produce enough to surpass our competitor. For the first time in 15 years, a non-corporate branch took home the premium trophy in the company. Unfortunately, it was not my branch, but we had an outstanding year in other areas.

Our agent, Joline Whiteman, wife of the then Minister of Education, Hon. Burchell Whiteman, and herself an educator and sports coach, was of great encouragement to me in the branch. She earned the Top Award for the best sales achievement in Group Business in the entire company. The branch was also leader in Group Business. I was now a fixture on the winner's podium at these awards banquets. But I was not finished. There was one prize that I had left, and I had to win, before I retired from the business.

I had a feeling that my hour was drawing near.

CHAPTER 14
MISSION ACCOMPLISHED

> *"It is not fair to ask of others what you are not willing to do yourself."*
> —ELEANOR ROOSEVELT

THE LIFE INSURANCE INDUSTRY was now booming, and the company had a field force of over 400 agents. Approximately 11 insurance companies were in operation and the company's ultimate goal was to become a Fortune 500 company.

In 1992, when realising my dream of taking the branch to the number one position seemed to be fading, I came up with an idea.

> I thought it would be wise to terminate all my non-performing agents. This would allow me to get a lower quota and give me a higher productivity rate and opportunity to get a higher percentage over the quota—key areas to score the points needed to win the President's Trophy.

In 1993, the President's Trophy fever was very much in the air. I planned my branch retreat early, before I attended the one at the company level as I really wanted to get my team off to a fast start. At the company's retreat, it seemed as if everybody wanted to win the coveted trophy that year. The reigning champion from Mandeville threatened to take it home again and boasted that our efforts were futile. I decided that this time around I would remain silent and let my performance do the talking.

We held our Annual Award's Breakfast and I planned a special treat for my agents. Over the years, an invitation to the Ocho Rios branch Awards was sought after by other colleagues. I don't know if they wanted a day off from the head office or our Award's event was just outstanding. I would like to think it was the latter. The agents left the Award's Breakfast feeling highly motivated. I promised the branch that if we won the President's Trophy for the following year, I would take everyone, including the administrative staff to the hotel of their choice, for a weekend to have our celebration and retreat.

I recruited a number of women on my staff. One of them, a young lady by the name of Leopatra Wallace from Jamaica National Building Society, gave up a supervisory position to work at our branch as a cashier, and for a significantly lower salary. She was a team player and not long after, she got an offer from another company for almost twice the salary she was being paid. She came to me seeking advice. I wanted her to stay but I recommended that she take the offer. A few days later she returned. She was staying, and I was very happy to hear that. She heard what the branch wanted to achieve and wanted to be a part of the vision. She later took charge of the Ocho Rios branch's administration and contributed significantly to the branch.

While the Presidential trophy consumed us at the company, on a personal level, my passion for cars burned bright. All my life, I've tinkered with them, repaired them, and rented them. Now I was in a position to drive the best. The thought came to me that it was quite some time since I had driven my favourite brand of motor vehicle. Since the near death accident I had with my second Mercedes Benz, I decided I would give the brand a break. The price of motor cars was now very high as the government had imposed a 260 percent tax on motor vehicles with an engine class of over 2,500 cc. I had no intention of going below that size as I always liked a car with power.

One day, I saw a custom-built Mercedes advertised for sale by the Nigerian Embassy and I was excited to inspect this car.

I fell in love.

Few cars with this engine size had a manual transmission. I negotiated with the ambassador to get a good price even though several other people were there trying to acquire the car. I finally got the ambassador to lower his price to US$35,000 which was the equivalent of a million Jamaican dollars at that time. I immediately called a friend who operated a motor vehicle valuation business. He told me the current valuation on the car was 1.9 million dollars.

I was ready to buy. The ambassador insisted on receiving the money in US currency. I had the impression that he thought I was wasting his time as I did not look like someone who could meet his demands. I quickly reassured him that I would be giving him a personal US dollar cheque for the car. He looked at me from head-to-toe several times.

It was almost 5pm on a Friday evening so he asked his chauffeur to quickly drive him to the Citibank on Knutsford Boulevard to validate the cheque. We arrived at the bank but it was closed for business. Recognising the ambassador, the security guard promptly opened the door. My bank in St Ann's Bay was contacted and the ambassador returned to where I was standing with a wide smile on his face.

"Mr Williams", he said, "the car belongs to you."

We went back to the embassy on Waterloo Road and he invited me in to his luxurious office. He suggested I take a bottle of wine from his collection and invited me to drop by whenever I came back to the city. I drove the car to the office in St Ann, and invited everyone to come outside and take a look. I was not boasting but wanted to show them what great possibilities they had if they delivered on their targets in this business. After all, this was my motivating factor when Tony Williamson recruited me as an agent from the beginning.

> *"If your actions inspire others to dream more, learn more, do more and become more, you are a leader."*—JOHN QUINCY ADAMS

Since I assumed the position of Branch Manager, I had suspended most of my personal selling. Although I was now leading the team and doing a good job, my first love was selling life insurance; large numbers of applications. I knew I was in the hardest fought battle for the President's Trophy. My personal production could give us added advantage in the race. I offered my own commitment to the team, expressing that I would be in the field with them helping to achieve their goals and that I would be producing enough to be among the best of them. We decided to have quarterly retreats to monitor what was needed to keep us way ahead of the competition.

MEMBERS OF THE OCHO RIOS BRANCH

During the year, many different branches took the lead at one time or another and everybody worked hard to gain ascendancy. In the last quarter, our little branch placed itself on the perch, in pole position in the company. (Pole position in motor sports is the position of the driver at the front of the grid in the starting line-up).

I was elated.

I vowed that whatever the other branches threw at us would not be anywhere near enough to make them win. My biggest rival and good friend, Tony Tomlinson from the Mandeville Branch, was in second place. Throughout the year, Tony and I continued to hurl competitive banter whenever we saw each other.

Speedy settlement of the applications became a priority. Good initial underwriting by the agent is the secret; ensuring all questions are answered properly and having all medical examinations completed were essential. On occasions, I directly called the clients to prompt them to do their medicals and fulfil other requirements. I was consumed with winning the top award.

By December 1993, the Ocho Rios branch was still leading, followed closely by Mandeville. Despite our lead, an extraordinary month from the Mandeville branch would put us in trouble. I did an analysis of what was required to put away my competitor: I worked out the average case size of the branch and realized we needed to settle 400 cases in the month to win.

I assembled my team to discuss what we needed to achieve. When I gave them my personal commitment to bring in fifty cases, they committed to the rest. I left the meeting in high spirits. In my first week in the field I sold thirty five cases. This had a great impact on the rest of the team at our Monday morning meeting. During the course of the month, my energised team produced so many applications that our administrative staff had to spend late nights processing them. I was not prepared to take any chances.

On December 21, 1993, the day before the books were closed, I spent the day at the head office making sure all the applications in the mill were progressing smoothly. I left Kingston late that day and was heading home to Discovery Bay but decided to drive by the office. To my shock, at 10:30 p.m. the administrative staff was still working. So fully vested were they in the branch's vision, I had to persuade them to go home.

The day of reckoning arrived and head office stayed open until late into the night. Wanting to realize another record breaking year, the company tried to process as much business as possible. On a branch level, only Mandeville could defeat us and I had been monitoring them very closely on the final night.

It was countdown time, filled with tension and anticipation. I sat at the computer for the final hour before the company closed off the settlement of its business. The New Business Clerk would take a policy number and settle one case for Ocho Rios and the same would apply for the Mandeville Branch. This went on for approximately thirty minutes and I discovered that all the other branches had completed their settlement for the year and it was just two non-corporate branches now going down to the wire.

PICTURED WITH THE PRESIDENT'S TROPHY

Cases continued to be settled for us but then I realized only Ocho Rios was taking numbers for settlement. My friend in Mandeville ran out of applications.

He was finished.

Mission accomplished! Ocho Rios won the President's Trophy for 1993.

The following morning, I went to the branch very early to kick start the celebration. The Lord knows how badly I wanted to win this competition and he had granted my request. By now, I had attained perhaps over one hundred awards since the beginning of my career but this was very special.

CHAPTER 15
TROUBLE IN PARADISE

"A hero is an ordinary individual who finds strength to preserve and endure, in spite of overwhelming obstacles." —CHRISTOPHER REEVES

1994 BROUGHT WITH IT NEW CHALLENGES to consider. In 1992, I travelled overseas to attend a management convention where the speakers warned of the changes brewing in the North American insurance industry. It occurred to me, that it was only a matter of time before there would be a ripple effect in Jamaica. I came home resolving that I would manage my finances in a more prudent manner. I would have to make sure that the gains I had reaped would last.

My family business, Salem Car Rental, was doing exceptionally well. I was now in the process of building a sixteen bedroom apartment/hotel on the main street in Runaway Bay and I was preparing to move the car rental business to a bigger location. I also had a plan to increase my fleet of cars to 100. I had made a promise to myself and my colleagues in 1978 that I would retire from the business in 1997 at age 45, and I was very much on schedule.

The country was experiencing high inflation and this was having a resultant effect on the insurance industry. The company survived by increasing the production level and made extra demands on the field force. Accordingly, we delivered any amount of new business that was required. This however could not continue.

The Jamaican dollar suffered from frequent devaluation against the US dollar. The black market thrived and there were minute cracks appearing in the financial sector. Interest rates on certificates of deposit also spiraled upwards, out of control. Although I benefited from this, I was very concerned. I knew that if this was to continue it would have a great impact on the insurance business as interest costs are critical to the operation of life insurance companies.

Our branch had its Annual Branch Awards Breakfast at the Jamaica Grande Hotel in Ocho Rios. It was a grand affair, and as I had promised in 1991, the guest speaker was the president, R. Danny Williams. What a great feeling and moment that was for me!

The company's Award's Breakfast was held a few weeks later, and every member of the branch, including both the sales and administrative staff, was invited. We were placed on a platform in the ballroom, set above and apart from all others. I can't recall ever witnessing anything like that in all my years of attending those events.

In addition, I received several awards for my own personal performance and a standing ovation when I was in the top ten of the most productive sales persons for 1993. It was a great moment for me and I can still vividly remember it as if it were yesterday morning. The news about my outstanding performance began to make the rounds and I received a number of invitations from within and outside of the company to share how I was able to deliver that remarkable performance. Previously, I turned down most invitations of this nature as I really did not like to speak about myself and, I didn't think I was good at public speaking. I have changed my position on that these days.

Despite the challenges in the economic climate, the life insurance industry experienced phenomenal growth in 1993 and this continued to 1994. We however saw changes in how the company was dealing with some of the benefits that were given to the sales representatives in the past. There were rumours that the company would rearrange its bonus system which I confess was the most generous of all the companies that operated in Jamaica. We observed that there were cuts in almost everything. News coming from other industry players was even worse than Life of Jamaica. It was about this time that I got a call from my colleague, Marvin Walters who was appointed President of the Unit Managers Association. His members were concerned about what was happening in the company and they would be very happy if I could brief them on the issue. I wrote the following speech and shared it with the group:

> There is good news about the industry now. The business is here to stay but as to the distribution of the product we need to prepare for a lot of changes. My advice to you is to get business-like for the next two years. Try to earn as much as you can and build a good cash reserve because things are going to change rapidly. These are a few of the things that you are going to see over the next two years:
>
> 1. Companies are going to get lean and mean.
> 2. There will be a lot of reductions in the field force as more emphasis will be placed on quality rather than quantity.
> 3. There will be a greater reduction in the number of units.
> 4. There won't be many companies to run to for a reprieve.
>
> There is no question that the agency system will be with us through the remainder of our lifetime. However, we could find a lot of our agents in the near future on the level commission system. I believe the future sales meeting between agent and prospects may soon occur via video telephone systems. In spite of all these potential changes that may be in our future, there is one thing that remains common- they all involve an individual salespersons interacting with a customer in the same way. Therefore, there is space for the unit manager, however our survival will be dependent on our ability to recruit and retain high calibre agents. I think the time has come for us to shift focus from the number of recruits and get concerned about the quality of those whom we seek to recruit.
>
> Ladies and gentleman, if we remember anything, I say remember the buzzword for your future survival in this business is quality recruiting.

We had a long discussion session and I could see that I had left a lot of people worried. It seemed that Earl Moore, the Vice President of Mutual Life Assurance Society, the oldest insurance company in the country had heard about my presentation. He invited me to speak at his company retreat which was to be held at the Boscobel Beach Hotel in St Mary, which was then owned by his company. He explained to me that he was having serious problems with his managers. His managers did a survey and found out that other companies were giving benefits they were not getting. He had explained to them that the company could not do anymore for them at the time but they would have none of it. He therefore wanted me to share with them what I spoke about at the Unit Managers' meeting.

He gave me the topic on which I should speak: "How I see the industry now and beyond the year 2000". I spoke to the Mutual Life group and warned them about what I thought was going to happen in the near future. I had written my address and delivered it, but I got a great urge to say something that I had not planned. I now felt it was the Holy Spirit and I had to say it. I said "You gentlemen and ladies say you are "The Giant of the Caribbean" (their tagline at the time) but the Giant of the Caribbean is going to stumble and fall. They did not throw me out of the hotel but I could see that it was not well received. Six years after I made that statement, I was introduced as a prophet at a Guardian Life retreat where I was invited to speak. Just two years after my address to the Mutual Life group, the company fell off the radar. It is now owned by Guardian Life.

> **"Business is like tennis; those who don't serve well will end up losing."** —AUTHOR UNKNOWN

The country experienced a near collapse of the financial sector following major fallout in the local stock market. We at Life of Jamaica witnessed the sudden decline in the value of our clients' investments.

Several of the policies we had sold them had an element of stocks attached. Many of our funds saw a rapid decline in their portfolio values and clients were encashing their investments for fear of further losses. I spent a lot of time in 1994 giving financial advice, reminding clients of the inherent risk and volatility of investments and why they should wait out the troughs. I wanted to stem a run on the funds which would exacerbate the decline in the fund values. Of course, being there for the clients would help to reassure them and reduce the ripple effect on the morale and productivity of the team.

The Universal Life policy, a top selling product introduced to the market in 1986 by the company, started to unravel. This was an excellent policy as it gave the applicant the best of both worlds; large sums insured and an opportunity to share in the company's investment fund. High interest rates and the fall of the stock market wreaked havoc on the actuarial projections. This caused my focus on new business to take a secondary position. However, the branch continued producing at a high level. Opportunities for advancement were still available at the company and being appointed Senior Branch Manager was a distinct possibility. Such a promotion would provide added prestige and a higher level of earnings. I thought this would be an ideal challenge as I would need the additional funds for my retirement in 1997.

After winning so many awards on a branch level as well as on a personal level, the next stage in my career development was to build a "mega-branch". This would see me doubling my manpower at the branch in two years, resulting in having sixty sales representatives. I was off to a good start with my recruitment drive and then I got the news that Life of Jamaica had purchased all the Jamaican operations of American Life Insurance Company and integrated their block of business into our operations. This led me to ask for additional office space in the building. This request was granted, arming me with the space to make my final dream at Life of Jamaica a reality.

Signs of cutbacks within the industry were clearly evident. All the new companies that had spent large sums of money to buy agents from other companies had started to send them away. Many of these agents found themselves with no place to go; all the companies were trimming their field forces. I realised I had made the right decision to stay with Life of Jamaica.

The country's financial woes in 1993 saw most financial institutions, including Life of Jamaica, with a mismatch of assets and liabilities. The press had a field day blaming the insurance companies for moving out of their core business and building larger head offices.

"Such ignorance!" I thought. Insurance companies had to make long-term investments for their clients and make preparations for administration to ensure the organisation's smooth operation. I am not at liberty to speak about what happened in other companies but as for Life of Jamaica, it was a well-run company and I can't recall ever getting anything for free. They were generous with how they paid their employees but you had to work very hard for it. However, when you borrow money at a 15 percent interest rate to fund your operations and then have to make repayments at 50 percent, even if you are the best manager in the world, you are going to face problems.

The company found itself in just this situation in 1995. While all this was happening, R. Danny Williams, the founder and beloved president of the company, announced he was retiring. I really felt sad as I reflected on all the hard work he had put in to build a company of the stature of Life of Jamaica, which gave ordinary Jamaicans like myself the opportunity to be anything we wanted to be. He appointed the young and bright Richard Powell, whom he had in training for many years, to succeed him. Powell immediately was thrown into the lion's den to take the company out of its current financial situation.

> **"We cannot solve our problems with the same level of thinking that created them."**—ALBERT EINSTEIN

The government of the day continued to progress on the same path and the financial situation gradually deteriorated accordingly. The United States dollar moved in value from being worth $22 JMD in 1992 to $40 JMD in 1996. I now figured my dream of building a mega-branch was essentially a pipe dream. The company was now left with no alternative but to cut staff, both at head office and from among the field force.

In 1996, I thought it would be motivating to attend the Million Dollar Round Table Convention being held in California that year. I was asked to serve as a host with the programme's general arrangements. My good friend, Aaron Greaves, and I stood at the convention entrance and ushered the more than six thousand attendees from all over the world to the ballroom each morning. This was a great feeling and it gave me a boost as I felt like I was a part of a remarkable industry.

Many Jamaicans were at the convention and one of the largest contingents was the Life of Jamaica attendees. I can remember there was a lot of discussion about the state of the company and the impending dislocations we would face. The new president of Sagicor, Richard Byles, was present and he had been invited as the President of First Life Insurance, the company he previously served in a similar capacity. He wasn't saying much as his company was the only insurance company that was not really troubled by the financial crisis. The Vice President of Life of Jamaica, Raymond Walker, also was present at the

MDRT CONFERENCE, JUNE 1996. ANAHEIM CONVENTION CENTRE, CALIFORNIA WITH AARON GREAVES (AT RIGHT) GUEST RELATIONS HOST.

convention. I observed that he left the convention before it had ended to return to Jamaica. Something was not right but I was having a good time and I refused to allow anything to rob me of my joy. I had nothing to worry about as I was prepared for anything.

I returned to Jamaica in June of 1996 to shocking news that Life of Jamaica and a number of other companies, in an effort to get their operations back on track, had approached the Jamaican government for financial assistance. The next shocking news was that the company was about to cut the total number of branches from 22 to six and return to its core business. I had expected some downsizing but could not have predicted that drastic cut. I took solace in the belief that I would not be affected as there was only one branch in Ocho Rios and I didn't think they would want to close it.

I later received a very disturbing surprise.

A great level of uncertainty loomed over the company and the insurance industry. I wasn't worried. I proceeded to carry out my business as usual, selling insurance and ensuring that my branch targets were met. The company soon sent a directive stating all agents who were performing below a certain level of productivity should be terminated. With the high cost of operating a branch and the company's financial situation, they had calculated the cost to keep agents and ensuring that the cost was maintained.

Many managers had served the company for years and had thought that they would have been able to stay and retire with dignity, but this was not to be. I got a call from a long-serving manager who told me that, enroute from Kingston to Montego Bay; a client informed him that he learned he was terminated and he later found out that his client was right. I thought this was very cold.

At this point I began to think seriously of leaving the company.

> **"In matters of principle, stand like a rock; in matters of taste, swim with the current."** —THOMAS JEFFERSON

One morning I was on my way to the office when one of my agents beckoned to me nearby the Breezes Hotel in Runaway Bay, owned by Life of Jamaica at the time. I pulled over and he proceeded to tell me he was very concerned about the Ocho Rios branch. He had attended an Agent Field Council Meeting and he was told that my management contract would be terminated and they were thinking of downsizing the branch to be a sub-branch of Montego Bay – again.

To me, that was the biggest joke of the century as the Ocho Rios branch was among the most productive in the company. I went home that night and thought of all the scenarios that could have occurred to lead the company to make this decision. I recalled that in June, when I had returned from the Million Dollar Round Table convention, my administrator said she observed uncharacteristic visits to the branch from certain members of the head office's management staff. Something seemed off about this and I now began to think a plot was brewing to expel me from the branch.

I was very uncomfortable and decided to call the company's Senior Vice President to speak with him about my future with Life of Jamaica.

> **"I like a little rebellion now and then. It is like a storm in the atmosphere."**
> —THOMAS JEFFERSON

I got the appointment to see my immediate boss and travelled to Kingston for the meeting. I really prayed and asked the Lord to help me keep calm and cool under all circumstances. I was walking along the foyer of the head office when a unit manager from the Halfway Tree branch informed me that a senior official of the company was losing his job and was desirous of taking over the management of the Ocho Rios branch. He also told me the person had devised a plot with one of my unit managers to say I was spending most of my time at my business in Runaway Bay, neglecting my responsibilities at the branch. Apparently, this same official had responsibility of making the decision to downsize the branch to the sub-branch level and appoint his accomplice, the unit manager, as the new manager of the branch. But when he became privy to the figures of the branches and realized the Ocho Rios branch was the pick of the non-corporate area branches, he wanted to have it as part of his portfolio. This official had already decided to close the Savanna-La-Mar branch and one of the two branches in Montego Bay.

Now he was planning to get Ocho Rios, regardless of the cost.

My spirit identified with what he said as there was evidence to support the claims. I was very pleased he had that amount of interest in me to see the need to tell me what was happening. Over the many years I had spent with the company, one of the things I cherished was the respect and encouragement I received from my colleagues. I always acted in a professional manner in all my undertakings, and as a Christian I made sure I kept my witness. I also knew I was loved by almost every member of the company. In spite of all that was happening I knew I had the good Lord as my Divine Saviour and the backing of the company's sales force—a group to whom I had given loyal service.

> **"The trouble with being in a rat race is that even when you win, you are still a rat."**—LILY TOMLIN

I proceeded to the Senior Vice President's office to discuss my future with the company. He invited me into his office and offered coffee, an offer I quickly declined as I only had one intention and that was to state my case. He informed me he was going through a rough period as he had to make some difficult decisions and some of the managers were not responding well to those decisions. Some of these managers had not properly managed their finances and were holding on for their lives. I hastily went on to tell him that I did not need the job and would be willing to leave but I was there because I thought I deserved some respect from the company. I was not pleased that news about my demise already was out in the streets before I was advised.

It seemed the company had not made a decision about Ocho Rios but it was standard procedure to look at all the branches. The company had no plan to close our branch, he reassured me. I advised him of the low morale in the branch and that the staff had heard about what was happening and had given me their assurances that they would leave the company if the rumours came true. He promised he would come to our branch to reassure them but I still left his office dissatisfied.

I returned to Ocho Rios the following morning to discuss what took place. I told them I was not willing to work with that unit manager and that if he were to stay then I would resign. I informed them I was responsible for all that the manager had achieved because I had brought him into the business and I was not prepared to have him as part of my team. The Senior Vice President later came to our office to discuss the matter with the other managers in the branch. The end result was the transfer of the unit manager to the Montego Bay branch. This news was now all over the company and my colleagues were very disturbed. I received a lot of calls and they told me they were monitoring what was taking place and if things continued the way they were going I could be assured I had their backing.

The news also came that the senior official had resigned hastily and this created a position for one of the previously terminated managers to get back his job as Manager of the Montego Bay branch. The Senior V.P. spoke to my agents about the work I had done in Ocho Rios and the good name I had given to the area. He affirmed there was no intention of changing management at the branch. I was pleased this was done as I always worked to maintain my dignity and I was not going to compromise it for anything at all.

The then-company president, Richard Powell, soon learned about what transpired. I had developed a good relationship with Richard during our time at the company as he was at one point the head of the company's Property Department and I liaised with him on several occasions to locate properties in St. Ann. On one occasion he asked me to help locate property to house a branch for the Jamaica Citizens Bank that he wanted to set up in St. Ann's Bay. He wanted the branch to be in a specific spot by the market but this was very hard to find. However, I convinced a policyholder to diversify his plan to change the ground floor to facilitate the opening of a branch of the bank. Unfortunately, the bank was taken over by The Financial Sector Adjustment Company (FINSAC) before this could have been realised.

FINSAC was enacted in the late 90s to strengthen and restructure the country's banking and insurance industries. But it was too late. The financial system had reached a state of considerable distress and investments of depositors, policyholders and pensioners were at risk.

So within this disquieting framework of shaky economic conditions, I had to contend with a nasty plot to remove me from my position. This was a very stressful period in my career as I could not believe that after all I had given to the company, someone could consider carrying out such a plan. However, I was very happy I still would be able to retire with dignity from the company where I had spent most of my working life. I had helped shape it to be one of the most successful companies in Jamaica and the wider Caribbean. The branch continued to have success in selling even though great uncertainty shrouded our operations.

Although I was assured by the president that the branch would be secured, the usual enthusiasm in the morning to get up and go was missing. I now started to do a complete analysis of my family business over the years. I had held back the growth of the company because my wife and I thought it best for her to focus on our children. By now though, they had grown up. My daughter was about to graduate from high school, my first son was in high school and my second son was at preparatory school. I wanted to make sure all of them could reach their academic goals and I had already calculated the funds it would take to do this.

Sometimes when you are running at the pace I was going you don't get to see how well you are doing. I discovered I had done an excellent job of managing my earnings from the life insurance business and I could make any decision I wanted as I did not have to work another day in my life. However, I did not want to make this decision on my own. I discussed the matter with my wife. I was not too worried about what she would say because I came to know that whatever decision I made she would support me. I really prayed to the Lord for a signal that would show me which decision to make. I had given no clues to my colleagues that I had any intention of leaving the business. I was sad because if I had to leave, my policyholders would miss the good service they had come to expect from me and the good relationships I had built would be no more. A thousand things flowed through my mind about what I should do and I really wanted to make the right decision. It was coming to the end of 1996 and my personal production was still at a reasonably high level and I had earned a good bonus. The branch also was doing well but, alas, a decision had to be made.

CHAPTER 16
THE END OF A MAGNIFICENT RUN

"Good friends are hard to find, harder to leave and impossible to forget."

"In the end it's not the years in your life that count, it's the life in your years." —ABRAHAM LINCOLN

ONE MORNING IN OCTOBER 1996, I was sitting in my office in Ocho Rios reflecting on the many cups, awards and trophies I had received. I wondered how it was possible to achieve all this in just 19 years with the company. It was like I heard someone say to me that it was time to go. I felt as if I was sleeping and I woke up from a dream.

I knew the Lord had spoken to me.

I immediately pulled out my blue letter pad and scribbled out my resignation, gave it to my secretary and dispatched it to the head office. I called my office assistant and told her she should find some boxes as I would be taking down my awards and plaques, packaging them and bringing them home with me.

The news began circulating around the office that I would be leaving the company and there were many sad faces. I really felt bad, especially for my Branch Administrator, Camille Warren, who I had recruited from her teaching career to lead my administrative team. They did a fabulous job and I was very grateful.

Later, I met with my immediate boss, Michael Fraser, and discussed the terms of my departure. He gave me encouragement and asked me to stay for the rest of the year to facilitate a smooth transition of the branch's leadership. I agreed and continued doing what I do best, selling a lot of insurance and helping the branch to another good year of production. It resulted in me getting my biggest management bonus, ever.

At the end of the year, Michael Fraser suggested he would give me an independent advisor contract to continue my relationship with the company, and I accepted. In the 1980s I was part of a group of super-producers who fought courageously with my good friend and former company president, Adrian Foreman, for us to receive a vested contract. The contract would allow agents who had exceeded a certain level of production to continue to earn renewal commissions, payable on the policies they had sold over their career, as long as the policy was still in force. I was now in a situation to continue serving the policyholders who had given so much to me over the past years.

I had now completed the last of my three goals I had set in January of 1978 at my first branch retreat at the Forum Hotel in Portmore, St. Catherine. I was a happy man to see that all my plans were accomplished, and I was onto the next challenge in my life. I would now be able to give my wife and children some of the time that I took away from them. I could ensure they did not experience some of the injustices I had to face because my father and mother were not in a position to provide for me. I would now be able to take on some more work for the Lord as I had more time at my disposal. Community work was also on my horizon. I always wanted be involved in giving back something to help the people of St. Ann, who had been very good to me.

> *"Every private citizen has a public responsibility."*
> —MYRA JANCO DANIELS

It was now 1997 and I had not realised before, the pressure I was carrying until I woke up in the mornings and did not have to hit the road early. I was planning to help my wife with the family business and spend time on some volunteer work in the community. I had built one part of a small apartment/hotel and now I was preparing to complete the other section. I was enjoying a good occupancy rate as we were selling a package with car and accommodation. The car rental service was doing extremely well.

I came to the conclusion that I would have to move to larger premises to accommodate the growth I envisaged in the near future. In achieving this, I would use the existing property to facilitate the hotel. I really did not want to become involved in anything that would use up a lot of my time as my plan was to look after my children and see to their education. Corporate board meetings now were replaced with parent/teacher meetings. I would also take my children to play tennis and my sons to play cricket, my favourite sport.

It seemed as if several organizations had heard about my retirement and I received calls from many schools and colleges. Several of them had seen the many times my photo appeared in the press and the things written about me, and wanted me to share my experiences. I did not like to talk about myself and I hated public speaking so I declined on many occasions. However, I would accept the invitations that had to do with life insurance, my expertise.

More community activities were in store for me. My friend, the Hon. Burchell Whiteman, asked me to serve on the board of my alma mater, Brown's Town High School. I accepted and soon was appointed vice chairman of the board. I was also approached by both political parties to run for office. On one of these occasions I was recruited by the head of the party himself. I declined in both instances. I really did not think I could fit into the type of politics that has been practised in our country. I was sorry I could not take on the opportunity to serve. In the 1970s, I was very active in politics and I have no doubt I would be sitting in Parliament if I had kept at it.

I also received an invitation from Pauline Haughton, who was a vice president of the St. Ann Chamber of Commerce, to join her in helping the chamber reclaim the vibrant position it had held in the parish. I had known Pauline for some time as she was a friend of the Ocho Rios branch and was always in attendance at my awards banquet to give support. I tried to get out of her invitation, but if you know Pauline well, this was difficult to accomplish. I joined the Chamber as a director and was invited to serve on the Finance Committee and the Cruise Ship Committee and was appointed as Chairman of the Membership Committee. The following year saw Pauline appointed as President of the Chamber of Commerce. I worked with her all over the parish to recruit business people to join the Chamber. This resulted in the St. Ann Chamber of Commerce being voted as the Best Parish Chamber of Commerce for three consecutive years. I was commended for my contribution to the Chamber's growth in membership. I was instrumental in identifying the grant to build the conference room at the Chamber's premises in Ocho Rios.

In addition to all the community work I was doing, I served on the board for the Jamaica Baptist Union Nutshell Conference Centre. I thought that after retirement I would have a lot of time for resting but I was more involved than when I worked. However, the difference was I now volunteered my services. I was also invited to serve at one of my favourite places, the Torado Heights Christian Centre in Montego Bay. As a young Christian, this was one of the places I would hang out with my peers for spiritual renewal. I had some wonderful times sharing in the ministry of Menzie Oban, his wife Winsome, and his children. I served as a trustee of their organization, Teamwork Associates, which operates a Technical Training Institute. I also chaired Teamwork Associates' Finance Committee.

In 1997, we continued to see growth in our car rental business. I was still searching for a property where we could expand as we now had more cars than our present location could accommodate.

At the end of December 1997, Life of Jamaica showed a profit of 92.1 million dollars, compared to a 1.1 billion dollar loss in 1996. I was happy for the turnaround as I really wanted the name of Life of Jamaica to live on forever. Richard Powell had now left office and Milverton Reynolds was appointed president, with the Hon. Dennis Lalor serving as the Executive Chairman of the board. The company was not really out of its problems yet as it would need some injection of capital. Company officials were waiting for the next injection of capital but this never materialised. It seemed the then Minister of Finance had a change of mind and the company was sold to Sagicor Life, a Barbadian company.

This was one of the saddest moments in my life.

I must say I have no problem with Sagicor Life as I am still associated with the company. They are doing a fantastic job under the leadership of the astute Richard Byles. Life of Jamaica was in my estimation, an exemplary institution and I am sure many people who worked there would attest to that notion. It was my university and I never could have accomplished any of my aforementioned feats with another insurance company. The training offered to employees was of a high quality. If you travelled to anywhere in the world and you met someone who worked at Life of Jamaica through the years, you would have met someone capable of doing extremely well. I think no accolade is too high to extend to the man who, through his love for country and mankind, sacrificed his time and finances to give us this opportunity. I am very happy the company's present head office was named to honour a truly great Jamaican businessman, the Hon. R. Danny Williams.

Fast forward to the year 2000; the market had many investment opportunities. I had some good real estate holdings that had escalated in value after I bought them at reasonable prices. I sold a few of those that I thought had peaked and would not realize any further capital appreciation. Thus, I had some cash at my disposal and I didn't have any great interest in putting any more capital in real estate.

I picked up the Jamaica *Gleaner* newspaper one morning and observed that the National Commercial Bank advertised a list of properties they were selling. I drove to Kingston just to find out if there were any properties being sold at a bargain price that I could buy and dispose of instantly. My car rental company had just purchased a property where I would house a new head office and I had started construction of a big garage. I still had plans of building an outfit that could accommodate 100 cars. I now had a fleet of approximately forty cars, all owned by the company, and without a loan from the bank. This really was a success story considering I started the business with no capital. A large crowd gathered at the hotel where the auction was being held, hoping for bargains. We all came to the conclusion that the properties were too expensive. I took my prospectus and went back to St. Ann.

I had it in mind to give the prospectus to my good friend and past associate Donald Fisher whom I had trained in the life insurance business but who was now a real estate broker. Fate would have it that on a Wednesday evening in June 2000, I saw him while I was passing his house in Discovery Bay. I quickly told him about the properties in St. Ann that he could get on his listing and handed the prospectus to him. He had a property at a bargain price for me but I didn't hesitate in telling him I was not interested in purchasing any more real estate. I had said that to him many times before, but he was relentless; I perhaps had given him too much training at Life of Jamaica. The listed property was Jamel Continental Hotel, a 24-bedroom hotel on the ocean front in Richmond, St. Ann. I had a little experience in the operation of accommodation facilities and did not like the business. I knew my wife was not interested in the business either but I made an enquiry about the selling price. I could not believe the low asking price. I expressed my wonder by asking him if the property was falling apart because I figured that would be the reason why it would be listed at that price.

The situation was the bank had seized the property for non-payment of a loan and had put it up for public auction but nobody could come up with the money. The bank really didn't want to keep it on their books anymore and had decided to do a fire sale. I immediately asked him to take me to the premises.

I had some knowledge of the hotel as I had taken the Ocho Rios branch there for a retreat. The experience and ambience of the property was excellent. We inspected the building, which then was operated as a health care facility. We both came to the conclusion that all it needed was a proper cleaning and a fresh coat of paint.

I was ready to make the purchase.

Just as I had expected, my wife told me I should avoid taking the risk. She reminded me that I was retired and this would be too much of a challenge at the time. What she said sounded logical under the circumstances but pride had come over me and I could not resist. I told her to prepare to go to Kingston with me as she would have to sign the documents.

The next morning, equipped with what was needed for the purchase, my wife and I proceeded to Kingston. I arrived at the bank to meet the person responsible for the sale. On arrival, I discovered that this person was a very good friend. She was so happy to see someone who wanted to buy the property as the bank was desperate to sell. Although the property already was being sold at a discount, my negotiating habits got the better of me. I made an offer that was 20 percent less than the asking price. She rebuffed the offer and indicated that the price had been reduced by 15 percent in the week before; hence there was nothing else she could do.

I conceded and told her I was ready to buy.

She responded happily and called the lawyer who was assigned to oversee the sale. He was in court at the time and, even though I told her I would come back another time, she insisted. She eventually got the lawyer to go to his office. When my wife and I got to his office, I realized the lawyer was the same man who was involved in the purchase of my first property several years before. We had met each other several times at the Kingston Cricket Club where we both had memberships. He hoped this was a final sale as he had done several sales agreements before but there was no conclusive action. He asked me where I would be securing the mortgage to make the purchase but I said I would be paying by cash. He thought I was joking and asked me again, just to be sure.

The documents could not be prepared without a commitment from the bank; so I called the bank manager in St. Ann's Bay. The two of them spoke and when they were through the attorney smiled widely. He told me he was going to get all the paperwork done on that day and after I signed and the bank manager sent him the required letter, the hotel would be mine. I saw the hotel on Wednesday evening and on the next day I was an hotelier.

My lack of expertise in the hotel business would have been a limitation but after my years in the insurance business, I felt invincible. I stripped the hotel and began to renovate and furnish it to the requisite standards. I opened the hotel's doors in six months' time and started to accommodate guests. In February 2001, I completed a course conducted by the St. Ann Chamber of Commerce in association with the Netherlands International Hotel Management, which was very helpful. We purchased properties on both sides of the hotel, which increased the capacity to forty-three rooms on three acres of seafront property, yet another success story. I now was doing what I wanted to do all these years, operating my own businesses. Operating the hotel in those early years was not easy, but I relished the challenge. I am grateful for the life insurance business that made all of my dreams possible. I really think a career in life insurance is the nearest a person can get to being their own boss.

I continued to service my clients under the new umbrella of Sagicor Life and during this period, I continued to get many invitations from a wide variety of organizations. I overcame my earlier public speaking inhibitions and spoke at colleges, seminaries, high schools, university campuses, insurance retreats, Chambers of Commerce retreats and several graduation ceremonies. Some of the topics included excellence, entrepreneurship, business management and my forte, salesmanship. I was also interviewed on various topics by several radio stations.

> *"We make a living by what we get, we make a life by what we give."* —SIR WINSTON CHURCHILL

On December 6, 2006, an article written by my former Branch Manager, Tony Williamson, under the caption "From Rags to Riches: How the Power of a Dream Propelled a Son of St. Ann," appeared in the *Daily Gleaner*. He spoke of how he nearly booted me out of his office when I came in for the interview. He said I did not fit the profile of the people he employed and he also spoke of the many records I broke. However, he left out a very important part as he did not say how well I paid him for all of what he did, something I found out for myself when I became a branch manager. Tony Williamson is, without a doubt, one of the best motivators the local life insurance industry has seen. He has produced some of the best salesmen in the insurance industry during the past three decades. He continues to speak all over the world, helping many individuals with the transition from failure to success. I know there is nothing he enjoys more than motivating people, and he is very good at it.

In 2008, I got a call from a senior journalist at the *Daily Gleaner*. She was doing a feature for Father's Day and I was selected to be interviewed for *The Gleaner's* Sunday Magazine, *Outlook*. I really was caught off-guard and could not understand what was happening. I asked why I was selected and not one of the many great fathers I knew in Jamaica. She told me she had the privilege of meeting my daughter, who was now a law student at the University of the West Indies, and my two sons, who were studying at the University of Technology. She was very impressed with the level of discipline and other good behavioural traits they demonstrated. She wanted me to share how I was able to raise them in this manner in our contemporary environment.

I agreed to have the interview and it was published in *The Gleaner's* Sunday magazine, *Outlook*, on the 28th of September in 2008. I am sure it was seen and read by many people in Jamaica, and possibly all over the world. I shared the spotlight with the Hon. Dr Usain Bolt, who was also featured for his heroic performance at the Olympic Games held that year. I could not escape the many calls of congratulations and commendation I was getting. Many people who knew me quite well told me they were surprised as they did not know I had done so well in my field of employment. I now was being invited to several functions to share my experiences. One of these occasions was in 2009 when I was invited as Vice President of the St. Ann Chamber of Commerce to attend a public forum put on by the then-Prime Minister of Jamaica, the Hon. Bruce Golding, at the Ocho Rios High School Auditorium. While there, I was introduced to the forum organizer, Ian Boyne, the acclaimed author, television personality and Jamaica Gleaner columnist. As soon as I was introduced to him he said he knew my name and realised I was associated with the life insurance business. He had interviewed several of my colleagues and said that he would be delighted to have me on his award-winning television programme, "Profile". I agreed but I was unsure if I wanted to appear on television to discuss what I had achieved.

I hoped he would have forgotten about the interview but, being the thorough journalist he is, he called to give me the date when he would conduct the interview. I thought about the matter and told myself that if this interview could help even one person to change their life, it would be entirely worth it. I turned up for the interview on the appointed date and was very impressed with the manner in which Ian conducted the interview. He really got me to say things that I would not reveal to my closest friends. When the interview was aired I received many calls from all over the island offering congratulations. I also got three calls from the Income Tax Department that week, apparently they wanted to collect another time.

> *"A man's real work is determined by what he does when he has nothing to do."*
> —MEGGIDO MESSAGE

As more invitations poured in for me to share my success story at various events, one invitation took me by surprise; a request from the Sagicor Production Club, which comprises all the top agents in the company. They had seen the "Profile" interview and thought I would fit in with their list of speakers for the annual Production Club Seminar, to be held that year at the Wyndham Rose Hall Hotel in Montego Bay. The first thought that came to my mind was to decline. My feeling was that, as a Life Member of the Production Club and the most successful life insurance agent in the company over the years, I had never before received an invitation to share my experiences with the group. The time drew near and I never had been a platform speaker for that forum before. The representative from the group called me on several occasions, and was very persuasive. I eventually yielded to their request and decided I would take the challenge. I did the appropriate research and prepared a speech suitable for the occasion. On arrival at the hotel, I was of the view that the seminar was only for my colleagues who were associated with Sagicor's operations in Jamaica. I was escorted to the ballroom where the main platform was situated. The ballroom was full, with hundreds of people from all the countries where the company operated. I must confess that my relative inexperience in speaking at that level made me a little nervous.

I made my presentation for one full hour and I was having such a good time that I exceeded my time by 15 minutes. The feedback from the audience was very positive. On my way out, I received a lot of commendations for the presentation. I also observed the presentation was recorded and was being sold to participants at the conference. It felt like an MDRT moment!

In 2010, the North Coast Times had a running series of features. The newspaper's owner, award-winning journalist Franklyn McKnight, selected me to be featured in a "Gentlemen Elevating and Motivating Society" (G.E.M.S.) feature. I thought this would be a good opportunity to say thanks to the people in the community who had contributed so much to my success in life, so I consented. I was featured in the paper and the response was very encouraging. I was now realising that my life was having a great impact on the many people I came across each day. It was during this time that my good friend and church sister, Marcia Gooden, a teacher at the HEART Training Institute in Runaway Bay, asked me to assist her. She needed help with selected groups of students in changing their way of thinking. I volunteered, and after speaking with the first group I realised that a lot of young people attend these institutions and then graduated without knowing where they are going in life. I worked with these groups over the years and was given a certificate of appreciation from the institution for partnering with them to change the participants' lives. I did this at a great sacrifice as I had several other engagements at the time, but it was time well spent.

I was now afraid to accept appointments to speak or to be involved in these activities as every time I was given an opportunity to speak, another person would call on me to share elsewhere. Additionally, the preparation needed for all these assignments was eating away at the time I would usually attend to my many other commitments, including my church responsibilities, which I never compromised. Over the years I was giving all this time and effort to the community for free. I really thought I owed this to the people of St. Ann, who contributed so much to my success in life. Everything I had done in my life had their full support and I will be forever grateful.

I can recall an incident that took place on my way to St. Ann's Bay. I was travelling from Richmond in my classic Ford Escort which I had not driven for quite some time. On reaching the entrance of the Seville Great House, I saw smoke coming from the bonnet of my beloved car. I quickly came out of the vehicle to investigate. When I opened the bonnet, I was greeted with a sweltering blaze that made me drop the bonnet. Even though the heat coming from the vehicle was unbearable, I tried to lift the bonnet again but it would not open. I now had resigned to the seeming reality that I would have to say goodbye to my favourite motor car. I looked around and I saw a lot of cars and pickup trucks approaching. The car is a popular fixture in St. Ann and on recognising it, people didn't hesitate in responding with fire extinguishers in abundance. Eventually the fire was extinguished and the result was that my car had minor damage. I was immensely grateful for their concern and support. I offered to compensate them for their kindness but they refused to accept any money from me. I was firmly convinced that St. Ann was the place I would continue to live and serve for the rest of my life as I felt the love from the people.

By 2012, it seemed as if my volunteer activities were having an impact. I got a call from the Custos' office informing me that as part of Jamaica's 50th Anniversary of Independence, an individual from each parish would be selected to honour their contribution to nation building. Several other criteria were mentioned and I was asked to submit my credentials to King's House. I had received so many awards in my short lifespan that I was not overly bothered about the outcome.

A few weeks later, I was selected for the Governor General Independence Award for Excellence for the parish of St. Ann. In November of that year I was invited to attend a special awards function at King's House commemorating our fifty years of independence. The Governor General gave me a beautiful plaque with the inscription: *"Excellence and Service are the hallmarks in the life of Leopold Williams of St. Ann, who has mentored and influenced many persons to achieve their individual goals."* I read the inscription often as a reminder of another mission that was accomplished.

ACCEPTING FROM THE GOVERNOR GENERAL THE 50TH INDEPENDENCE AWARD FOR EXCELLENCE IN THE PARISH OF ST. ANN.

The St Ann Chamber of Commerce

In September of 2012, the St. Ann Chamber of Commerce held its annual General Meeting where I was unanimously voted as President for the ensuing year. I had served on the executive committee for many years and had skilfully avoided the position of President. I did not have the time required to provide effective service as I still had to run my business, which was going through difficult times. However, my colleagues insisted I should serve. I accepted the challenge and quickly began to work.

Over the years, the community had rallied for improving the general town infrastructure of Ocho Rios and addressing the tourist harassment issues. As a result, I invited the Minister of Tourism, Dr Wykeham McNeill, and members of his ministry to a stakeholders meeting. Dr McNeill responded promptly and a meeting of all the chamber members and stakeholders was convened. Serious discourse followed, between the Minister and the business community, about the situation and he promised to provide a solution for each issue.

After many other meetings between the relevant parties, we began to see results. The Minister invited us to attend a meeting where a comprehensive presentation was exhibited regarding the development of the sidewalk and roads that led to and from the Cruise Shipping Pier.

My service at the Chamber of Commerce was fulfilling. One of the highlights was co-hosting the local radio station programme, "Justice" with the bright and beautiful Justice Marlene Malahoo-Forte at an outside broadcast in Ocho Rios.

The Chamber also hosted a very successful luncheon in Ocho Rios where they discussed the preparation for the proposed Logistics Hub. It was hailed as one of the most successful quarterly luncheons organized by the Jamaica Chamber of Commerce. I now was a regular fixture on radio and television, providing information about what was happening in the parish. This consumed almost all of the time I had for my other engagements. My colleagues wanted me to serve for another term but, unfortunately, I had to step down. I am not opposed to the idea of serving another term and when I am completely retired I may opt to make myself available for the position.

> *"Good deeds speak for themselves;*
> *the tongue only interprets eloquence."*
> —ANONYMOUS

In 2013 I was invited to speak at an Optimist International luncheon in Ocho Rios but I declined as the event was to be held on a Sunday. I always declined speaking engagements on a Sunday; unless it was in my church. The president of the club in Ocho Rios, who is my very good friend, rearranged the programme time to facilitate my coming in the afternoon after I attended church. I accepted the invitation and gave an address to the group. I never rated myself as a good speaker, especially in comparison to some of ones I have been around all my life. I have listened to some of the best in Jamaica and in the world but I am aspiring to be one before I leave the earth. Reporters from the newspaper outlets were present and my full speech was published in the Jamaica Observer newspaper.

A few days later I received a call from a Guyanese gentleman who was living in California. He told me he read the speech and was impressed with what I said. He told me he was writing a paper on Jamaica to present to a group of concerned Jamaicans in the Diaspora. Some of the things I said were similar to what he was advocating. He was married to a Jamaican woman and had developed a great love for the country and was coming to visit soon. He reminded me that I spoke of creating a foundation to help needy students to finish their education and he would help in that regard.

A few weeks later he invited me to come and see him and his wife at a hotel where he was staying in the area. He handed me a beautiful case which he brought me as a gift. He also gave me a copy of his paper which he had presented to the group. This has been a good reference point for me on several occasions. He also reconfirmed that he would be willing to provide financial assistance when my foundation was established. I had learned of the power that a good speech can have. My former boss and good friend, Tony Williamson, can unreservedly say that his investments in me were justified. If I need to, I can now make a living from motivational speaking.

CHAPTER 17
THE POWER OF MOTIVATION

"Motivation will always beat mere talent."
—NORMAN RALPH AUGUSTINE

I BEGAN TO REALISE THE IMPORTANCE motivation plays in the life of an individual. While I was active in the life insurance business, I used to ask myself why Life of Jamaica spent so much money on retreats and seminars to drill and rehearse the sales force, and then compensate them so well. My short time of sharing my experiences with various groups gave me the answers. I was invited by members of my church's youth group to share in a session regarding careers. Each year they invite individuals from different professions to provide enlightenment on the topic.

I chose to speak to the group on the topic: "Pursue Excellence". I really wanted them to understand that, regardless of the career opportunity that should come their way, if they did not perform with excellence they would not make a success of their lives. The presentation was well received by the group. It was followed by a question and answer session. A bright young man who was a recent university graduate said that while he was at university he had the opportunity to do research on the career of a life insurance salesman and was fascinated by the financial possibilities the career presented. He went on to say that he didn't think he would want to enter the field as it seemed crowded. He asked me if I thought anyone else could make it in the field. I quickly replied there was room at the top as all the crowding or bundling takes place at the bottom. He gave me a smile and I knew I reached him.

I had seen so many people enter the life insurance business and fail that I really started to wonder what was the cause. It occurred to me that they were not motivated enough to overcome the many obstacles a salesman faced. In my time as a salesman, there were instances where I would leave motivational seminars with the eagerness to put what I had learned into practice. I was very charged and no obstacles could derail me from reaching my goals. I have seen engineers, accountants, behavioural scientists and others, with an array of qualifications, who failed to last more than a year in the life insurance business. I have come to realise that the life insurance field is not a 100 metre dash. It is a marathon race that requires a lot of discipline, "stick-to-itiveness" and good old fashioned hard work that most people are wary of. Someone rightfully said the only place success comes before work is in the dictionary. I am a true believer in this adage. Too many people heard they could make a lot of money in the industry but were not prepared to do what was required to achieve this. The only problem I did not encounter as a life insurance man is a company telling me I sold too many policies and so they could not pay me. The resources never ran out. That is marvellous and it is for this reason that if I had the opportunity to start over and select a career, it indisputably would be the life insurance business. There is an old colloquial proverb that says "encouragement strengthens labour", and I believe that motivating persons to do what is necessary to succeed is the foundation of that saying.

> *"That some achieve great success is proof to all that others can achieve it as well."*
> —ABRAHAM LINCOLN

A Very Special Young Man

Many years ago I went into my bank to transact some business. A very enthusiastic young man came across the counter to deal with my transactions. I immediately realised that there was something that separated him from all the other clerks in the bank. My first thought was that if he had a little more experience, I immediately would have recruited him to sell life insurance. His attitude was infectious. I soon developed a close association with him as anytime I came into the bank he would take care of me. I began to encourage him and share motivational thoughts with him. I observed that he was getting promoted quite frequently and whenever he got a promotion, he would call me and I would give him some direction about where he should aim for next.

I went to the bank one morning and he was now in his own office as he was the Personal Banker for the branch. He would need my help as he wanted to make a good impression on the branch management. I gave him all the help I could and our relationship was enhanced when he married the daughter of my friend and agent, Bevon Lalor. I watched this young man work diligently to market the bank's products and he won many of the bank's island-wide awards. His sales ability was recognised by the company. Without any management training he was recruited by the bank's insurance arm and promoted to Regional Manager. The name of this young man is Kevin Ingram.

Following his promotion, he asked me to come to Kingston where he wanted to gather his sales force so I could inject them with some of my magic touch. He subsequently won many awards for his outstanding performance. I then advised him that if he wanted to reach the top, he would have to enrol in some course of study. He promised he would, and his continued high performance got him an offer to come back to St. Ann's Bay to manage the branch he had started at after leaving high school. He accepted and began his tenure as Branch Manager of the National Commercial Bank's St. Ann's Bay branch. He called me to say he had taken my advice and enrolled in the Manchester Business School with the aim of acquiring a Master's Degree in Business Administration. He quickly stamped his class on the St. Ann's Bay branch and was eventually promoted again to a bigger branch, this time in May Pen, Clarendon. The branch subsequently experienced phenomenal growth.

He recently was identified as someone who would be an asset to the National Commercial Bank's Capital Market arm and was promoted to Vice President of Wealth Management. I have no doubt in my mind this young man is going to the top of his organization as he lives, drinks and eats banking and is passionate about winning. What is the reason why this young man achieves this level of success while his more qualified colleagues still remain at the teller position? He developed a habit of hard work and determination to overcome whatever things were thrown at him—and there must have been many.

> **"Many of life's failures are people who did not realize how close they were to success."**
> —THOMAS EDISON

Juices Anybody?

A man of the Rastafarian faith used to sell his fruits at the corner of a petrol station with a cart stocked with fresh Jamaican fruit. He would shout in a loud voice, "mangoes", "bananas", apples", and so on. You could hear him from far away. One afternoon a truck drove around the corner and hit his handcart. The fruits spilled and the truck's back wheels crushed them. A crowd of people stood there expecting the Rasta man to spew out some expletives. However, they were surprised when, as the juices started to run down the road, the Rasta man shouted out "Juices anybody?!"

When everything around us crumbles, we don't need to get bitter, we need to get better.

I will share another experience from my motivational catalogue.

The Young Policeman

Oniel Brooks was a young policeman, just transferred to the Runaway Bay Police Station. He was a quiet character and was always neatly attired. I was not surprised when he was recruited by Mutual Life Insurance Company as a life underwriter. He told me he made the career change because he was impressed with what he saw when I came to the station to visit my clients and the quality of cars I drove at a young age. He had a very successful sales career.

Later on, I tried to recruit him to Life of Jamaica to be one of my unit managers but this was not to be. It seemed as if his company had gotten wind of my approach and promoted him to a similar position within their organisation. Today, he is a Regional Branch Manager at Guardian Life Limited. Some years ago in his capacity as a branch manager, he invited me to his branch's retreat to share my story with his team. I made my presentation, speaking about the insurance career and how it had changed my life. It was not until many years after, when I saw a young man who had attended the retreat, that I came to know the impact of my speech on him.

Touching Other Lives

I was coming from the Donald Sangster International Airport in Montego Bay, and my daughter asked me to stop at a food establishment in Ironshore. While I was at the counter ordering the meal, I heard someone calling my name. A handsome young man approached me but I had no recollection of him and asked him to remind me who he was. He told me he remembered me from the

Guardian Life retreat in Ocho Rios and he never could forget the speech I gave that day. He was about to resign from the business as he was failing and had decided he would attend the retreat, which in his eyes would be his last. While he was there he heard me say something about the insurance field that hit him very hard. He decided he would stay and apply some of the sales ideas I had recommended. I asked him where in life he was now. He had done well for himself and had retired from the life insurance business. He now owned and operated a pharmacy in Montego Bay and was exploring the opportunity of establishing another one. I jokingly told him he owed me a lot of money. I drove home from Montego Bay with a great sense of joy knowing I was able to rescue that young man possibly from the jaws of failure. If only more people could just hang in there. Who knows what changes they could realise in their lives?

When I started my life insurance career I was an ordinary, unassuming young man. I went back to my alma mater, Brown's Town High School, to see if I could get some of my past teachers to purchase insurance from me. I was about to enter the teachers' room, which was situated next door to the administrative office, when I heard someone shouting my name. A lady who knew me from my days as a student heard I was now in the insurance business. She told me I had better find something else to do as I could not make it in the business and was destined to fail. I was very embarrassed as everybody was laughing at me. I did not say a word, though, and proceeded to do what I came to do. The following year my performance led me to become the number one agent in the company. I visited the school again that year and the same lady shouted at me again. This time she was very excited. She told me she had seen my picture in The Sunday Gleaner and that she didn't know I was doing so well. I hope she learned a vital lesson for the rest of her lifetime, and that is to never put anyone down in the way she did me.

> *"To be a champ you have to believe in yourself when nobody else will."* —SUGAR RAY ROBINSON

In Spite of the Worst Situations...

I heard of a story: In a hospital, a doctor asked another doctor for his opinion on the termination of a pregnancy. In this case the father of the unborn child had syphilis and the mother had tuberculosis. Of the four children who were born to the couple, the first was blind, the second died, the third was deaf and mute and the fourth also had tuberculosis.

"What would you have done?" The second doctor said,

"I would have terminated the pregnancy." The first doctor replied,

"Then you could have murdered Beethoven," Said the second doctor.

We all know the impact Beethoven's symphonies have had on the world of music. Even the worst of situations can lead to great opportunities in life.

To Give Up or Not to Give Up...

In my own family, I want to share two examples of one who gave up and another who didn't. The first example is about my participation in athletics while at Secondary School, competing in both the 100 metres and the relays. I was very quick and had the talent to become a top athlete. I represented my school at the inter-secondary meets that were held at Richmond Estate just across from where my hotel is now located. I was involved in a meet at the York Castle High School playing field, running the anchor leg in a relay.

Later in my life I learned a great lesson about not giving up from my beloved niece, Deon Hemmings. Deon grew up in the district of

Minard Hill in Brown's Town. She was the second child of my sister, Dimple Williams, and Leonard Hemmings, now deceased. They were in no way wealthy but they raised their children with a lot of discipline. Deon attained a scholarship to attend the York Castle High School and developed a liking for athletics. She wanted to become a champion athlete but this proved to be very challenging. At that time, a rural school didn't offer many opportunities or support for students to make the transition into becoming top athletes, but she persisted. She participated in many track meets in the parish and at the National Boys and Girls Athletics Championship. She did not win many of these races but she was determined that she would eventually reach the top. She caught the eye of top sports administrator Pat Anderson, who was responsible for promoting sport in his company and, to a greater extent, Jamaica. He took her to Mandeville and brought her into his own home and made her a part of his family. He also took on the task of training and motivating her. She chose to specialize in one of the most difficult events in track and field, the 400 metre hurdles.

In 1992, at the age of 23, the Barcelona Olympics presented her with a taste of what was to come. She placed seventh in the finals of her event but, despite not receiving a medal, the press saw something in her. She was tipped as one of Jamaica's hopes for a gold medal at the 1996 games, held in Atlanta. I developed a close relationship with her during this time. I can remember many times when she told me she would be taking home the gold. I still have some of the souvenirs she would take back to me after her feats at track meets she participated in all over the word. There was a particular moment in December 1995; just months before she would be crowned champion, that really inspired me. Her mother, who lives in Miami, was home for the Christmas holidays. She invited close friends and family to have a celebration for her outstanding performance so far and for what was to come. We had just gathered to bask in the delicious food her mother had prepared at the family home in Minard Hill when Deon announced the sad news that she had to leave to head to Mandeville for training. The crowd that gathered, and those yet to arrive, were very disappointed as they did not get to see enough of her and hear more from her. I now realize the level of determination

MY NIECE, DEON HEMMINGS, WINNING GOLD AT THE 1996 OLYMPIC GAMES IN ATLANTA.

and motivation this young lady had at the time. She went on to the Atlanta Games in the summer of 1996 and won the 400 metre hurdles in an Olympic record time of 52.82 seconds. When she came home following her accomplishments, I had the privilege of driving her from the Norman Manley International Airport in Kingston, and what an experience that was! I had a few anxious moments when I thought my beautiful Mercedes Benz was going to disappear in the jubilant throng of people assembled along the road from the airport to New Kingston, where she would be staying. On arrival at the Jamaica Pegasus Hotel, where her family was staying as well, we were escorted by a limousine to Jamaica House. Everybody who was anybody in Jamaica at that time had gathered to welcome her home. She was the first woman in Jamaica and the wider English-speaking

AT DEON'S HOUSE DURING A FAMILY DINNER IN BROWN'S TOWN

Caribbean to win an Olympic gold medal, and her celebration was the biggest I have ever seen for an athlete. She later went on to win silver at the Sydney Olympic Games in 2000 and establish herself as one of the finest female hurdlers in the history of the Olympics. Shortly after her heroic performances, she resigned in 2003 and married Mike McCatty. She later gave birth to her son, Mikael. She and her husband now own a real estate company and reside in Mandeville.

It is quite evident that a life that is motivated can do what most would think is impossible. Who knows what I could have accomplished on the track if I had the tenacity of my niece?

CHAPTER 18
THE FUTURE

"The trouble with the future is that it usually arrives before we are ready for it."
—ARNOLD H. GLASGOW

I MUST FIRST OF ALL GIVE THANKS to the Lord God Almighty for what He has done over the past forty years in my working life. There was nothing prior to my acceptance of Him as my Lord and Saviour in 1973 that would have indicated any assurance of a fruitful and successful life but through His divine grace, He granted me a very purposeful life. It has been a life full of high moral principles that served me well through my many years in the life insurance business, where the standard of morality was not the best. I must also thank the many people who helped me achieve the many milestones I have been fortunate to attain. I will be forever grateful to my dear mother, Eliza Williams, and my father, David Williams, for their sacrifices and the love and discipline they instilled in me. Their efforts had a great impact in shaping me into the man I am today. I wish they could be here to see what their son has turned out to be. I am sure they would be very proud.

I am indeed also thankful and bless the Lord God for the gift of a beautiful wife and three children. My daughter Patrice has completed two separate stints at the University of the West Indies, attaining a degree in International Relations and in Law. She successfully completed her studies at the Norman Manley Law School and now practices as an attorney. My sons Andrew and Kirk both attended the University of Technology where they completed studies in

THE FAMILY (FROM LEFT): SON, ANDREW; WIFE, DIANA; MYSELF; DAUGHTER, PATRICE; AND SON KIRK.

Business Administration. I am now looking forward to motivating my grandchildren to even higher levels of success than I experienced.

I must confess I am not worried about what tomorrow has in store because I know who holds the future, and as long as I continue to serve Him, my future is assured. However, I know He has given me wisdom to function while I am here on earth and I will have to apply it to survive in this world of uncertainty. When you speak with many people on the streets and our young children, they will tell you there is no future for Jamaica. If you look at how many of our leaders and politicians operate, you would want to agree with them, but my view asserts that the future is determined by their actions. When I started out in my career 40 years ago the future was just as challenging as it is now. As a matter of fact, I think the contemporary standard of living supersedes that of the past. More children now are able to enjoy higher levels of educational opportunity and upward social mobility than when I was growing up. If we tell ourselves that things are going to get worse then what we say will come to fruition. We must always maintain a positive attitude. Let us look on some of the excuses we make for not succeeding in life. A lot of people in Jamaica today are using the race card to stay in a state of poverty. They are still trying to say they are oppressed by their former slave masters. Don't get me wrong, I think the enslavement of our people is one of the worst things that occurred in history, but we must move on and take our rightful place in the future.

> *"[Jesus said], Everything is possible for one who believes."*
> —MARK 9:23 NIV

> *"Excellence is to do common things in an uncommon way."* —BOOKER T. WASHINGTON

One of my favourite movies is the classic "Gone with the Wind", which saw Vivien Leigh portraying the role of Scarlett O'Hara and Clarke Gable as Rhett Butler. One thousand four hundred women auditioned for the coveted role of Scarlett O'Hara. The film was released in 1939 and received thirteen Academy Award nominations. It won ten Oscars, including Best Picture, Best Actor (Clark Gable), Best Actress (Vivien Leigh) and Best Director (Victor Fleming). An African-American woman by the name of Hattie McDaniel also became the first woman of colour to be nominated for and win an Academy Award. She received the Best Supporting Actress Oscar for her portrayal of Mammy, Scarlett O'Hara's slave.

"Gone with the Wind" became the highest earning film made up to that point and held the record for a quarter of a century. It remains one of the most successful films in box office history. The film was criticised for its historical revisionism and glorification of slavery but, surprisingly, was credited with bringing changes to the ways African-Americans were depicted in film. What a lesson to those of us who find excuses for our lack of excellence in our everyday life. In that era, there weren't many black women who were given a starring role in films as they were only cast as domestic workers. She had previously acted 309 times as a domestic worker but this time out performed herself in her role as "Mammy". At the Academy Awards presentation in 1940, she was not allowed to sit with her acting contemporaries due to the racial segregation that existed at the time. She had to sit at a table at the back of the room. Her performance yielded her the Oscar for her supporting role in the film and she also became the first woman of colour to speak at the awards ceremony. She was overcome with emotion and ran off the stage, bursting out in tears. Since then, many black people have been nominees and recipients of Oscar awards.

We must not allow the negatives we hear to control our thinking. It was our own Bob Marley who popularised the saying, "Emancipate yourself from mental slavery, none but ourselves can free our mind". I had times in my teenage years when I wished I would not have to face the future. All of the things I wanted to accomplish as a child had eluded me and my life was a seeming failure. "Thanks be to the Lord" as He showed me there was hope, and I realised my destiny was in my hands. It was when I came to this realisation that I was able to move from failure to success with His enabling. A lot of negative people exist today who can't, or at least refuse, to see or speak about anything positive. I have tried my best to avoid being associated with them and instead identify with men and women who are successful. I encourage young people to do the same. Additionally, they should know what they want in life and set an attainable plan to get there. I really did not depend on wishful thinking or waste time dwelling on failure. There is a real challenge for our young people today to carve out a successful future in this ailing economic situation. Many of our young people are finding it very difficult to complete their education. And, even after their parents make the sacrifices to pay their way through tertiary institutions, there are very few employment opportunities. As the wise man Solomon said in Ecclesiastes 1:9, "There is nothing new under the sun." and that resonates with our situation here. Economic uncertainties and many other issues are always ever present. When I was faced with this reality, I researched the lives of people who were able to overcome the odds and succeed. Today, whenever I come up on anything challenging, I still replicate that formula. If you were to do some research, you would discover that most of the present Fortune 500 companies were formed in a time of economic depression. Many of the world's most successful people reached the apex of their chosen disciplines because of the difficulties they faced in their life or country. Remember, the only thing that is constant is change.

Mahatma Gandhi is a great example of a man who, through his selfless acts, not only liberated his own country but is a source of inspiration to many others. Born on the 2nd of October, 1869 in Porbandar, India, Gandhi was a mediocre student but his parents encouraged him to study law. In 1888, he went to England to attend the University College of London to become a barrister. He returned to his homeland to set up a legal practice but did not do well. He got a one-year contract in 1893 to work at a law firm in South Africa. During his tenure at the law firm, he saw and suffered racial discrimination. It was there he coined the term "Satyagraha", which signified his theory on non-violent resistance. In 1915, he went back to India to take on the injustices inflicted on his people by the British. He was arrested and tried for sedition and sentenced to imprisonment several times. He used the non-violent approach to later bring independence to his country in 1947. Gandhi's principles laid the foundation for two extraordinary men who, through the same method of non-violence, went on to liberate their respective nations. The first was Martin Luther King, Jr. He was an American pastor, humanitarian and leader of the African-American civil rights movement. He organised several non-violent protests, including the 1955 Montgomery Bus Boycott, and also helped organize the 1963 March on Washington, where he gave his "I have a dream" speech. He developed a reputation as one of the greatest orators in American history and, in my opinion, "I have a dream" was the greatest speech ever delivered. He was investigated and profiled by J. Edgar Hoover as a Communist. This could not stop the man on his mission to end racial inequality in America. However, he paid the ultimate price for his determination to free his people from racial tyranny. In April 1968, King was planning a national march on Washington D.C. to be called "The Poor People's Campaign." He was assassinated on April 4 in Memphis, Tenn., where he had gone to support striking black sanitation workers. Today King's mission is not completely finished but we have clear evidence of the work of this great man. We have the first black President in American history in office, and others that hold key positions in the country.

The second man who was inspired by Gandhi was Nelson Mandela, the great South African son. He was born into the Thimbu royal family in 1918. He attended Fort Hare University and the University of Witwatersrand where he studied Law. While living in Johannesburg, he became involved in anti-colonial politics, joining the African National Congress (ANC). He became a founding member of the organisation's Youth League and came to prominence in the ANC'S 1952 Defiance Campaign. He secretly joined the South African Communist Party and sat on its Central Committee. Although he was committed to non-violent protesting, he led a militant protest against the apartheid government in 1962. He was subsequently arrested and convicted for conspiring to overthrow the state and sentenced to twenty-seven years in prison. It was there the world saw the courage of this great man and lobbied relentlessly for his release. He was eventually released in 1990 and then engaged in negotiations with the then-President to abolish the wicked apartheid system and establish multi-racial elections. He led the ANC to victory and served as South Africa's first black President. He became even more respected in the world because of his stance for peace and reconciliation in South Africa. We can see how the example of one man who took a stance to save his country motivated others to do likewise.

When you study the lives of these great men, it inspires one to "be the change you wish to see in the world" as Gandhi states. I cannot leave this world without contributing something to our beautiful country where the Lord has blessed me to live.

In Jamaica we are having our own problems as our economy has experienced less than one percent annual growth over the past 40 years. We had a grand celebration for our 50 years of independence in 2012, but it is estimated that we have experienced the lowest average growth rate in the Americas. Since the year 2000, even the poverty-stricken country Haiti did better than that. The Chinese, who are having their run in the country at this time, have a proverb that says: "Each generation will reap what the former generation has sown." We unfortunately only have debt to pass on to the next generation. It was the aforementioned J. Edgar Hoover, former head of the U.S. Federal Bureau of Investigation and menace to Martin Luther King, who said, "Blessed are the youth, for they shall inherit the national debt,"—a truly profound statement which is very much appropriate for our current situation. It is for this reason I will spend the rest of the time the Good Lord gives me to do something about it.

> **"Education is the most powerful weapon which you can use to change the world."**
> —NELSON MANDELA

With the idea of effecting change, I have launched the **Steely Williams Foundation** with a mission to help young people complete their education. I will continue motivating and mentoring to the best of my ability. I will be mobilising others in Jamaica and the Diaspora to help secure the future of our young people. We must all help, in whatever way we can, to create a bright future here in Jamaica—this beautiful paradise island we call our home.

ACKNOWLEDGEMENTS

1. To Tony Williamson for giving me the opportunity to join his team as he was not certain I could have made it and to his wife Jean, for treating me as part of her family.
2. To Desmond and Mauva Smith for insisting that I stayed in the Life Insurance business and inviting me to live in their home to guarantee their support.
3. To Pastor Denzil and Lorna Vaughn for their encouragement and for being true friends.
4. To the Hon. R. Danny Williams for offering great advice, placing confidence in me and providing a company of Life of Jamaica's calibre where I could finish my business education and earn a good living.
5. To my Pastor, Everard Allen and his wife Myrna, for their spiritual guidance and personal support towards my success in the Life Insurance business.
6. To Pastor Menzie and Dr Winsome Oban for their personal support and spiritual guidance during my early years.
7. To Herbert Hall for great support and advice during my early years at Life of Jamaica.
8. To my best friend, Vincent Reid for just being a true friend.
9. To my son, Kirk for his exemplary commitment and skill in doing the initial editing and typographical work on this publication.
10. To my editors, Lena Rose and Michelle Neita for their encouragement, understanding and high level of professionalism.
11. To my children Patrice, Andrew and Kirk for making parenting easy.

12. To my Doctors, Professor Michael Lee and my friend and family physician Dr Phillip Henry for keeping me healthy to face the many challenges I have had to overcome.
13. To all the members of the Brown's Town Baptist Church for their love, fellowship and support over the years.
14. To the memory of my colleague Ossie Lannaman and my friend Dr Cindo Nicholson.
15. To Tommy James for his help in providing historical material for this book.
16. To my wife, Diana, for her continued support.
17. Finally to the Lord and Saviour for His enabling over these years.

ABOUT THE AUTHOR

Leopold Williams, popularly known as "Steely," is one of the most outstanding life insurance sales professionals and managers in the fields of life Insurance and business in general. Leopold was recruited into the insurance industry, at the age of 21, after only two years of working in both the private and public sectors.

He celebrates 40 years in the life insurance industry and has established himself as one of the most prolific salesmen in the three companies he represented throughout his career. He broke all the existing production records at Life of Jamaica and was the company's leading agent. He then went on to pioneer the opening of the Ocho Rios Branch on the North Coast of Jamaica. Appointed Unit Manager in 1986, Leopold became the leading Unit Manager in 1989 and the company's leading Branch Manager in 1993. He qualified for all insurance industry awards and is now a Life Member of the prestigious Million Dollar Round Table, where he has been a member for over 35 years. He continues to serve as a Senior Independent Financial Advisor at Sagicor Life Insurance Company.

As a way of giving back, Leopold has addressed attendees at conventions, sales retreats, seminars and groups from tertiary institutions on various topics including financial management, entrepreneurship, salesmanship and business management. He has also mentored several groups of students at the Runaway Bay Heart Academy.

Along with his success in the insurance business, he formed two successful companies: Salem Motors Company Limited, which has operated Salem Car Rental for the past 26 years; and Seacrest Resort Company Limited, which operates Seacrest Beach Hotel, a 41-bedroom hotel on the ocean front in Richmond, St. Ann., Jamaica.

Leopold has appeared in print media, on television, on radio programmes and is actively involved in community activities. He was President of the St Ann Chamber of Commerce, a member of the Finance Committee and Chairman of the New Membership Committee. He is also a Justice of the Peace and serves as a Lay Magistrate in the Children's Court.

As founder of the **Steely Williams Foundation** to help under-privileged children complete their education, Leopold is committed to service. In addition, he continues to mentor groups of young people in many institutions to achieve their personal goals. In recognition of his stellar contributions, the Jamaican Governor General presented Leopold with a commemorative 50th Anniversary Independence Award for his contributions to nation building.

An avid Christian, Leopold worships at the Brown's Town Baptist Church where he serves as:

- Cell (Small Group) Leader
- Chairman of the Property Committee
- Member of the Finance Committee

He is married to Diana Dawn Williams and is the father of three children, Patrice, Andrew and Kirk.

www.ingramcontent.com/pod-product-compliance
Lightning Source LLC
Chambersburg PA
CBHW070334180426
43196CB00049B/2209